W9-CDA-447

GANDHI AND HIS CRITICS

By the same author

Mahatma Gandhi – A Biography
The Nehrus
Gokhale, Indian Moderates and the British Raj
The Moderate Era in Indian Politics
Socialism in India (editor)

GANDHI
AND HIS CRITICS

B. R. NANDA

Wingate College Library

DELHI
OXFORD UNIVERSITY PRESS
BOMBAY CALCUTTA MADRAS
1985

Oxford University Press, Walton Street, Oxford OX2 6DP

London Glasgow New York Toronto
Delhi Bombay Calcutta Madras Karachi
Kuala Lumpur Singapore Hong Kong Tokyo
Nairobi Dar es Salaam Cape Town
Melbourne Auckland

and associates in
Beirut Berlin Ibadan Mexico City Nicosia

© Oxford University Press 1985

Filmset by South End Typographics, Pondicherry
printed by Rajbandhu Industrial Co., New Delhi 110066
and published by R. Dayal, Oxford University Press
YMCA Library Building, Jai Singh Road, New Delhi 110001

Contents

To Baba

Preface

'The man who became one with the Universal Being'—this was the sub-title of Romain Rolland's book, *Mahatma Gandhi*, published in 1924. 'One thing is certain', Rolland wrote, 'either Gandhi's spirit will triumph, or it will manifest itself again, as were manifested centuries before, the Messiah and the Buddha.' Twenty years later Albert Einstein could write of Gandhi: 'Generations to come, it may be, will scarcely believe that such a one as this ever in flesh and blood walked upon this earth.'

Magnificent as such tributes were, they would be misleading if they created the impression that Gandhi's career was a triumphal procession. Indeed from the day he plunged into the vortex of the racial politics of Natal until his assassination fifty-four years later, he was continually in the centre of one storm or other. In South Africa he was flayed in the European press and jailed by the colonial government; in 1897 he was nearly lynched by a white mob in the streets of Durban. After his return to India he incurred the inveterate suspicion and hatred of the British authorities. 'It is very necessary throughout', Lord Willingdon, the Viceroy, wrote in 1933, 'to view Gandhi as he is and not what he poses to be.' As late as 1946 Lord Wavell confided to his journal that Gandhi was an 'exceedingly shrewd, obstinate, double-tongued, single-minded politician.' The British rulers of India tended to see in him an irreconcilable enemy of the Raj, to suspect a trap in every word he uttered and a trick in his every action.

Gandhi had to contend not only with the guardians of the British empire. He never lacked opponents in his own country and indeed in his own party. He was the *bête noire* of orthodox Hindus who were infuriated by his denunciation of caste exclusiveness and untouchability and by his advocacy of secular politics. In the course of his Harijan tour he narrowly escaped a bomb attack in Poona in 1934; fourteen years later he fell a

victim to the bullets of a Poona Brahmin who charged him with
betrayal of the Hindu cause. Curiously enough, for years Gandhi
had been branded by protagonists of Pakistan as 'the Enemy
Number One of Islam'. Within the Congress Party Gandhi had
continually to cope with rumblings of discontent. He was repudiated by the older leadership of the Congress in 1919. In the
nineteen-twenties and thirties young radicals in the Congress
such as Jawaharlal Nehru, Subhas Bose and Jayaprakash
Narayan were straining at the leash: they fretted at the patient
and peaceful methods of the Mahatma. The Indian communists
dubbed him a charismatic but calculating leader who knew
how to rouse the masses but deliberately contained and diverted
their revolutionary ardour so as not to hurt the interests of
British imperialists and Indian capitalists.

Gandhi was patient with his critics. Through his weekly
journals and innumerable letters to his correspondents (ninety
volumes of his writings have already been published) he kept up
a continual dialogue with them. In November 1929 when
Jawaharlal Nehru regretted his signatures to the manifesto
issued by Indian leaders on Lord Irwin's declaration on dominion
status, Gandhi wrote to him: 'Let this incident be a lesson.
Resist me always when my suggestion does not appeal to your
head or heart. I shall not love you the less for that resistance.'
Gandhi encouraged his critics to come out in opposition so that
he could attempt to carry conviction to them or, alternatively,
change his own stand.

In the first chapter I have referred to certain comments on
Gandhi made in the wake of the Attenborough film, but in this
book I am not responding only to these comments. Indeed
much of the criticism is a repetition of what was said earlier
about Gandhi, even in his lifetime. Nearly four decades after his
death it should be possible to see Gandhi and his times in better
perspective. I have posed in this work some major issues which
have been brought up and tried to examine them in the bio-
graphical and historical contexts. Though my approach is
broadly thematic I have not been oblivious of chronology. I
shall feel amply rewarded if this book helps those who wish to
delve a little deeper into Gandhi's life and thought, and at the
same time want to steer clear of deification as well as denigration.
They are likely to discover in him a degree of rationality,

radicalism and relevance to our times which they may not have suspected.

I would like to thank Dr S. R. Mehrotra and my son, Naren, for taking the trouble of going through the whole manuscript and making useful suggestions. Professor T. N. Madan was kind enough to read two chapters. I am indebted to my wife for reading and commenting helpfully on every chapter as it was being written; without her encouragement and support I could hardly have started much less completed this book.

B. R. Nanda

CHAPTER 1

The Gandhi Film

The mystique of a box office hit is probably as elusive in the world of films as the mystique of a best-seller in the world of publishing. Who could have predicted that a film on Gandhi, thirty-five years after his death, would run for weeks in theatres packed to capacity from one end of the world to the other?

I shall not discuss Attenborough's film here, but it is possible that its extraordinary popularity was due to the fact that its release happened to coincide with one of those periodical spurts of the 'peace movement' which the growing menace of a nuclear holocaust has triggered in recent years. But this very coincidence has provoked a sharp reaction from those who dislike and distrust the peace movement and fear that it will weaken the will of the 'free world' to fight the cold, and probably the hot, war. For some of Attenborough's critics the eight-Oscar award proved the last straw. They reacted by assailing not only the film but also its hero, and there has been a spate of articles ridiculing and belittling Gandhi. Perhaps the most virulent attack appeared in an American magazine, *Commentary*, by the magazine's film critic, Richard Grenier.[1] As a film critic Grenier was perfectly within his rights to differ from the film juries who dispensed a whole series of awards to Attenborough and his team. But Grenier's qualifications for pontificating on Gandhi and the Indian nationalist movement are not clear.

The Indian revolution which culminated in the independence of the subcontinent in 1947 is likely to be as richly documented as the French and American revolutions. The records bearing on British rule and modern Indian history are almost an inexhaustible quarry for historians. The *Collected Works of Mahatma Gandhi* run into ninety volumes. The papers of the Indian National Congress and other political parties, the correspondence of Indian leaders, the back-files of newspapers and journals, and the reminiscences of men and women who made history (which are available in the Nehru Memorial Museum and Library in New Delhi) constitute a massive collection. Then there are government records in New Delhi and the capitals of the states of the Indian Union. In Britain the India Office Library, a vast repository of official printed and manuscript materials, also houses the private papers of viceroys, secretaries of state, governors and senior British officers who served the Indian empire.

The author of the article in *Commentary* is blissfully ignorant of these source materials; for his indictment against Gandhi and the Indian national movement he seems to have drawn on a couple of secondary works and travelogues. The article teems with half-truths, quarter-truths and untruths. From criticism of the film its author passes on to an attack on Gandhi, on Hinduism and on India. What shall we think of an Indian film critic who, after seeing a film on Abraham Lincoln, fired off a broadside against Lincoln, Christianity and the United States without knowing very much about them? We discover the cause of Grenier's indignation when, in the last part of his article, he ridicules Attenborough for his 'muddled pacifism' and for 'scrambling his way' to 'the heights amongst high-minded utopians, equalitarians and deliverers of the oppressed'. Evidently, Grenier is worried lest, thanks to the Gandhi film, peace may break out!

It is surprising that this astringent mixture of pique, prejudice and ignorance should have been eagerly lapped up by scores of newspapers and journals in the United States, Britain, Canada, Australia, the Middle East and the Far East. 'Responsible' newspapers and journals which would hesitate to accept an article on Tolstoy, Roosevelt, Churchill or Mao Zedong, except from a recognized authority, readily opened their columns to almost anyone—novelists, short-story writers and free-lancers— who cared to cock a snook at Gandhi. The certitude of these commentators seems to have been directly proportional to their ignorance of the subject. For most, it was perhaps their first and last piece on Gandhi, but they merrily joined in denigrating him and in suggesting that the real Gandhi was not a great man at all, that his ideas were impracticable, his methods ineffective, his achievements non-existent.

Whatever the motives for this campaign, it has done one good thing: it has after many years renewed the debate on Gandhi, and this time the debate will not be confined to a coterie of scholars.

Curiously enough most of the criticisms, the doubts and distortions provoked by the film, are repetitions of what was said about Gandhi in his lifetime. It was only natural that in the heat of controversy his political opponents should have painted him in the worst possible colours. He never lacked critics even in his own party who chafed under his moral straitjacket and grumbled against his patient, peaceful methods.

Every important figure in history, be it Cromwell, Napoleon or Bismarck, has been subjected to periodical assessments and reassessments. This is a game which historians and biographers play and which their elitist readers in every generation watch. No practical harm is done to the world around us by a distorted image of Cromwell's Irish policy or Bismarck's diplomacy. But it is different with Gandhi. His life, his thought and his methods have, as we shall see in the succeeding pages, a contemporary significance which we can ignore only at our peril. It is important, therefore, to set the record straight, not only to do justice to the memory of an extraordinary man, but to see if it has any insights for beleagured humanity today.

CHAPTER 2

'A Hindu of Hindus'

Gandhi's critics have had a field day, sneering at his 'saintliness' and his pursuit of 'personal holiness, at the expense of public good'.[1] We are told that he was 'a Hindu of Hindus', that his religious ideas are of little real relevance to the world of today.

What is the truth in this picture of Gandhi? What kind of religion did he profess and practise? And what effect did it have on his public life?

Curiously enough, though Gandhi grew up in Porbandar and Rajkot in western India in a devout Hindu household steeped in Vaishnavism and was exposed to strong Jain influences, his acquaintance with religion, even with the religion of his birth, was of the meagrest, when in 1888 at the age of nineteen he arrived in London to study law. It was with some embarrassment that he confessed to some English theosophist friends, who invited him to read Sir Edwin Arnold's *The Song Celestial*, that he had never read the *Bhagavad Gita* in Sanskrit, or even in Gujarati, his mother tongue. This was his introduction to a book which was to become his 'spiritual reference book'. Another book of Sir Edwin's, *The Light of Asia*, also fascinated him; the story of the Buddha's life, renunciation and teaching stirred him to his depths.

While the literature of the Theosophical Society was quickening Gandhi's interest in religion, a fellow vegetarian enthusiast introduced him to the Bible. The New Testament, particularly the Sermon on the Mount, went straight to the young Gandhi's heart. The verses, 'But I say unto you that Ye resist not evil; but whosoever shall smite thee on thy right cheek, turn to him the other also. And if any man will sue thee at the law, and take away thy coat, let him have thy cloke also', reminded him of the lines of the Gujarati poet Shamal Bhatt, which he used to hum as a child:

For a bowl of water give a goodly meal
For a kindly greeting bow thou down with zeal;
For a simple penny pay thou back with gold;
If thy life be rescued, life do not withhold.
Thus the words and actions of the wise regard;
Every little service tenfold they reward.
But the truly noble know all men as one,
And return with gladness good for evil done.

The teachings of the Bible, the Buddha and Bhatt fused in the young Gandhi's mind. The idea of returning love for hatred and good for evil captivated him; he did not yet comprehend it fully, but it continued to ferment in his impressionable mind. Before he left England in 1891, he had already outgrown the phase of atheism into which he had strayed in early adolescence.

During his first year in South Africa in 1893, Gandhi came across some ardent Quakers, who perceived his religious bent, and decided to annex him to Christianity. They loaded him with books on Christian theology and history; they preached at him, and prayed with him and for him. Finally, they took him to a Protestant Convention in the hope that mass emotion would sweep him off his feet. It appeared to Gandhi's Christian friends that he had been on the brink of conversion, but, for some unknown reasons, had stepped back. The first impact of Quaker proselytizing in a strange country was doubtless strong on him, but he was in no greater hurry to become a Christian in Pretoria than he had been to become a Theosophist in London. His knowledge of Hinduism was yet superficial. While books on Christianity and Islam were easily available in South Africa, he had to send for books on Hinduism from India. He sought the advice of his friend and mentor, Raychandbhai, a Jain savant of Bombay, who counselled him to be patient and to seek in Hinduism 'its unique subtlety and profundity of thought, its vision of the soul and its clarity'. His scholarly exposition reinforced Gandhi's own sentimental bond with the religion of his birth, and proved decisive during the period when his Christian friends believed him to be on the way to baptism.

Years later, Gandhi confided to a group of Christian missionaries: 'Hinduism as I know it entirely satisfies my soul, fills my whole being and I find a solace in the *Bhagavad Gita* which I miss even in the Sermon on the Mount.' He did not, however, accept every Hindu tenet or practice. He applied the 'acid test of reason' to every formula of every religion. When scriptural sanction was cited for inhumane or unjust practices, his reaction was one of frank disbelief. The oft-quoted text, 'for women there can be no freedom', ascribed to Manu, the ancient Hindu law-giver, he regarded as an interpolation, and if not, then he could only say that in Manu's time women did not receive the status they deserved. Similarly, he lashed out against orthodox Hindus who supported untouchability with verses from the Vedas. 'Every living faith', he wrote, 'must have within itself the power of rejuvenation.'[2]

Gandhi's Hinduism was ultimately reduced to a few fundamental beliefs: the supreme reality of God, the unity of all life and the value of love (ahimsa) as a means of realizing God. In this bedrock religion there was no scope for exclusiveness or narrowness. It was in his view a beauty of Hinduism that 'in it there is a room for the worship of all the prophets of the world. It is not a missionary religion in the ordinary sense of the word . . . . Hinduism tells every one to worship God according to his own faith or *Dharma* and so it lives at peace with all religions'.

The study of comparative religion, the browsing on theological works, the conversations and correspondence with the learned, brought Gandhi to the conclusion that true religion was more a matter of the heart than of the intellect, and that genuine beliefs were those which were literally lived. This was something beyond the grasp of those who had acquired, in the words of Swift, enough religion to hate one another, but not enough to love one another. Gandhi's first biographer, the Reverend J. J. Doke, wrote in 1909 that Gandhi's views were too closely allied to Christianity to be entirely Hindu; and too deeply saturated with Hinduism to be called Christian, 'while his sympathies are so wide and Catholic that one would imagine he has reached a point where the formulae of sects are meaningless'.

In his lifetime Gandhi was variously labelled: a Sanatanist (orthodox) Hindu, a renegade Hindu, a Buddhist, a Theosophist, a Christian and 'a Christian-Mohammedan'. He was all these and more; he saw an underlying unity in the clash of doctrines and forms.[3] He chided Christian missionaries for their 'irreligious gamble' for converts. It was the way a man lived, not the recital of a verse, or the form of a prayer, which made him a good

Christian, a good Muslim, or a good Hindu. The missionaries' bid to save souls struck him as presumptuous. Of the aborigines and hillmen of Assam he said: 'What have I to take to [them] except to go in my nakedness to them? Rather than ask them to join my prayer, I would join their prayer'. To a correspondent, who had urged him to save his soul by conversion to Christianity, Gandhi wrote, 'God is not encased in a safe to be approached only through a little hole in it, but He is open to be approached through billions of openings by those who are humble and pure of heart'.

Gandhi's religious quest did not lead him—as sometimes happens in India—to a cave in the Himalayas. He did not know, he said, any religion apart from human activity; the spiritual law did not work in a vacuum, but expressed itself through the ordinary activities of life. This aspiration to relate the spirit, not the forms of religion to the problems of everyday life runs like a thread through Gandhi's career: the slow unfolding and the near failure of his youth, the reluctant plunge into the politics of Natal, the long battle against racialism in South Africa, and the vicissitudes of the three decades of the struggle against British imperialism.

CHAPTER 3

The Making of the Mahatma

In his late twenties and early thirties, while Gandhi was engaged in his religious quest in South Africa, his life had undergone a remarkable transformation. From the Hindu scripture, the *Gita*, he had imbibed two ideals: 'non-possession', which set him on the road to voluntary poverty, and 'selfless action', which equipped him with an extraordinary stamina for public life. He trained himself as a dispenser in a charitable hospital in order to be able to attend on 'indentured' labourers, the poorest Indians in South Africa. At Phoenix near Durban (and later, at Tolstoy Farm, near Johannesburg) he set up little colonies where he and a few friends, who shared his ideals, could find a haven from the heat and dust of towns, away from men's greed and hatred.

These changes in Gandhi's mode of life entailed much strain on his wife, Kasturba. With her husband's increasing involvement in public life, she found herself running a veritable boarding house for his professional and political associates. The family savings were sunk in public causes. The household itself was shifted across two continents in response to the calls of public duty: a cablegram could send Kasturba and the children voyaging down to Durban from Bombay. Gandhi was outgrowing, 'private' life. Already in South Africa, his family came to include, besides his wife and children, numerous co-workers and followers, who had cast in their lot with him. As a practising Indian barrister, he could perhaps have secured the admission of his children to European schools. But he would not accept for himself as a favour what was denied as a right to his countrymen in South Africa. His children had to content themselves with such scraps of instruction as they could get from their father as they walked with him the ten miles to and from his office in Johannesburg. These peripatetic lessons were often interrupted by clients or colleagues; but despite their mother's protests, Gandhi refused to send his children to European schools. Inevitably, the education of the children suffered. The worst sufferer was the eldest son, Harilal, who later turned alcoholic. Gandhi's other sons, Ramdas, Manilal and Devdas, led normal lives, although they did not draw the spotlight of publicity, which from time to time fell upon Harilal and made him a life-long embarrassment to his parents. Gandhi publicly assumed responsibility for the mental and moral disintegration of Harilal. One wonders what to make of this parental guilt; there have been other eminent men whose children went astray and it never occurred to them to take all the blame for this misfortune on themselves.

II

We may now come to a subject on which much ignorant and even malicious comment has been made—Gandhi's concept of *brahmacharya* (self-control). Not only has this concept been ridiculed, but doubts cast on his own practice of it. To understand the evolution of Gandhi's ideas on this subject it is necessary to see it in the context of his own life.

Gandhi was married at the age of thirteen in accordance with, what he described as 'the cruel custom of child marriage'. The custom was almost universal among Hindus in the nineteenth century. The *Autobiography* records with a mixture of candour and regret the story of the boy-bridegroom. Gandhi was in his late fifties when he wrote this book; it is evident that the record of his teens seemed to him unedifying in retrospect. The frankness of the *Autobiography* has, however, helped to foster an exaggerated impression that in those early years he had let himself go. As George Orwell reminds us in a perceptive essay written in 1949, Gandhi offered in his autobiography a full confession of the misdeeds in his youth, but in fact there was not much to confess: 'a few cigarettes, a few mouthfuls of meat, a few annas pilfered in childhood from the maid-servant, two visits to a brothel (on each occasion, he got away "without doing anything"), one narrowly escaped lapse with his landlady in Plymouth, one outburst of temper—that is about the whole collection'.[1]

The autobiography takes the readers into confidence on a few escapades into which the young Gandhi was pitchforked in his youth. Mehtab, a school-mate, responsible for most of Gandhi's youthful misadventures, took him to a brothel. 'I was', he recalls, 'almost struck blind and dumb in this den of vice. She lost patience with me and showed me the door with abuses and insults'. Again, one evening as a student in England, he fled from a bridge party in Plymouth to his room, 'quaking, trembling with beating heart like a quarry escaped from its pursuer'. On his first voyage to South Africa, he was taken by the captain of the ship to an 'outing', which included a visit to Negro women's quarters; he recalled later that he came out as he had gone in.

It is significant that in all these incidents, while he allowed himself to be led into the very jaws of 'sin', he came out unscathed. It appeared to him that the grace of God—or good luck—had saved him. In fact, the odds were always heavy against his succumbing. As he trembled on the brink of temptation, there were powerful influences tugging at him. One was the monogamous ideal he had cherished since his childhood, the other was the vow to avoid meat, wine and women, a vow he had taken to obtain his mother's consent for his trip to England; and finally, his own shyness. 'If I did not talk', he wrote about his life as a student in England, 'no girl would think it worth her while to enter into conversation or go out with me'.

All the sins of his boyhood and youth, which filled Gandhi with remorse in later life, were thus committed within the bonds of matrimony. Here, too, the cycle of his sex life appears to have completed itself too soon. Between the age of thirteen, when he was married, and eighteen, when he left for England, his wife was with him for scarcely three years, having spent the rest of the time, as was the custom, with her parents. And when he returned to India after qualifying as a barrister in 1891, he was continually on the move in search of a living. He had scarcely spent six months with his family, before circumstances compelled him to leave in 1893 for South Africa on his own. 'The call from South Africa', he records, 'found me already free from the carnal appetite'; he was then only twenty-four. Not until 1896 did his wife and two sons join him in Natal. Three years later, he had already made up his mind to limit the size of his family.

Since he had already been opposed to the use of contraceptives, the decision amounted to the adoption of a virtually continent life. In 1906 he took the formal vow of celibacy (*brahmacharya*).

Henceforth Gandhi and his wife were bound by many bonds but excluding the characteristic one of marriage. They were at this time a well-adjusted couple; in their thirties they had outgrown the bickerings of their teens. Their life came to be less and less of a 'private life' and shaded into community life. Kasturba stood beside her husband as he courted insults and imprisonment during his struggle in South Africa; without her courage and support he could hardly have withstood the storms of public life. But it was not easy for her to accept the austere life he imposed on himself and those nearest to him. In 1901, as the family was about to leave for India, Gandhi was loaded with gifts of jewellery from his grateful countrymen. The idea of accepting valuable gifts for public service was repugnant to him, and he decided to put the jewels in a trust fund for the service of the Indian community in Natal. Kasturba, not yet free from the feminine fascination for jewellery, pleaded in vain with her husband to let her keep at least one necklace which she particularly fancied, but Gandhi would not budge an inch on, what was to him, a point of principle.

One evening in 1904, while Gandhi was taking a train from Johannesburg to Durban, a friend gave him Ruskin's *Unto This Last*. He sat through the night and read the book from cover to cover. When the train reached Durban next morning, he had already decided to reduce Ruskin's theories on the simple life to practice. A few months later when Kasturba arrived at Phoenix Farm, her husband's blueprint for an idyllic life, her surprise and irritation were obvious. She had long since reconciled herself to dispensing with gold necklaces and diamond rings, but it required some effort to give up even a modicum of comfort, and to turn herself overnight from the wife of a barrister into that of a peasant. Gandhi records that when he told her in 1906 that he wanted to take the vow of life-long *brahmacharya* she did not object. She had already consented to the metamorphosis of their external surroundings; she also accepted the renunciation of the sexual bond between man and wife. The occasion for the *brahmacharya* vow was the Zulu Rebellion in 1906 in which Gandhi led an Indian volunteer ambulance unit. During the strenuous marches through the 'solemn solitudes' of the kraals of Zululand, it was borne in upon him that if he was to devote himself to public work, he would find himself unequal to the task if he remained engaged in the pleasures of family life and in the propagation and rearing of children; in a word, he could not live both after the flesh and the spirit. The life of the flesh had in fact already diminished to zero.

Never again did Gandhi seek privacy with his wife or with any other woman. His life henceforth was an open book. He had no bedroom of his own; he lived amidst his secretaries, disciples and colleagues; their beds or mattresses were spread next to his. There is no reason to doubt his claim that he had attained full control over his conscious thoughts and actions. His rare 'lapses', to which he occasionally refers in his letters or articles, occurred in his sleep. He was deeply distressed if he had an erotic dream, and insisted on publicly expressing his feelings of shock and guilt. It was his ambition to banish carnal thoughts not only from his conscious, but from his unconscious mind. He regarded this total 'self-purification' essential if he was to keep himself a fit instrument for spiritual progress or for the service of his fellow men.

Forty years after he had vowed himself to abstinence from sex, Gandhi asserted that his wife and he had 'tasted the real bliss of married life' when they renounced sexual contact. 'It was then that our companionship blossomed and both of us were enabled to render real service to India and humanity in general. Indeed, this self-denial was born out of our great desire for service'.[2]

III

Gandhi would have agreed with the Pauline dictum that it is better to marry than to burn, but he regarded marriage as a sacrament in which sex was the least important factor. He advised continence even to those who were married, and considered sexual life 'physically harmful and morally sinful', unless it was for the express purpose of procreation.

A famous contemporary and one of the formative influences of Gandhi's youth, Tolstoy had preached similar views about the place of sex in human life. 'Men survive earthquakes',

Tolstoy wrote, 'epidemics, illness and every kind of suffering but always the most poignant tragedy was, is, and will be, the tragedy of the bedroom'. After the publication of *Kreutzer Sonata*, Tolstoy affirmed that the Christian ideal of love of God and one's fellow men was incompatible with sexual love or marriage, which amounted to serving oneself. Uncharitable critics said that the author of *Kreutzer Sonata*, the father of thirteen children, was getting old, and that the grapes had turned sour. In fact, for many years after he pledged himself to continence, Tolstoy was torn by an inner struggle of which there is plenty of evidence in his diaries. Not until he was eighty-one—a year before his death—did he feel free from sexual desires.

Tolstoy's struggle for continence not only strained his own moral and spiritual reserves, but shattered the already weakened vessel of his marriage. His wife was hysterical. 'I want to kill myself, to run somewhere, to fall in love with some one', moaned Sonya. Their life became a round of recriminations and reconciliations. Tolstoy's diaries round off the story of one of these quarrels with the terrible judgement: 'Between us there is a struggle to the death. Either God or no God'. His wife was totally unable to appreciate, much less to adopt, the ideals of her husband.

The changes which Gandhi brought into his life were no less radical, the ideals which he formulated for his family were no less revolutionary than those of Tolstoy. That the Gandhi household bore the stress better was due as much to the skill of the husband as to the sacrifice of the wife; she followed in the 'footsteps of her husband', however much it went against the grain. To her husband's 'reforms', her reactions were successively those of bewilderment, opposition, acceptance, conversion and championship. Whether it was the removal of untouchability or the wearing of homespun 'cloth', it was not at first easy for her to adapt herself to her husband's views, but when she did, it was done thoroughly, and she even preached them to others. Tolstoy's wife called her husband's disciples 'dark, dark people, pharisees, cheats, dissemblers'. Kasturba was able to treat her husband's disciples like her own children.

IV

Gandhi held that the true purpose of marriage was intimate

friendship and companionship between men and women, but sexual contact was permissible only when a couple desired to have a child. Margaret Sanger, the leader of the birth-control movement, who came to see him at Wardha, failed to win his approval to the use of contraceptives. Gandhi argued that if men and women could indulge in sex without having to suffer the consequences of their action, it would rob them of the faculty of self-restraint.

Gandhi's concept of *brahmacharya* presumed a certain approach to life. A man who had 'killed the sexual urge in himself', he wrote, 'would never be guilty of it in any shape or form. However attractive a woman may be, her attraction will produce no effect on the man . . . . The same rule applies to woman'.[3] He conceded that such self-control called for constant vigilance and effort:

> The vast majority of us would want to marry, to have children and generally to enjoy ourselves . . . but there are . . . exceptions to the general rule. [Some] men have wanted to live a life wholly dedicated to the service of humanity, which is the same thing as serving God. They will not divide their time between the rearing of a special family and the tending of the general human family . . . . [They] will be celibates for the sake of God and . . . renounce the laxities of life and find their enjoyment in its austere rigours. They may be 'in the world', but 'not of it'. Their food, their business . . . their recreation, their outlook on life must therefore be different from the general.

Thus, for Gandhi, the control of the sex instinct was part of a larger discipline of body and mind; it included not only freedom from desire, but from thoughts of desire. *Brahmacharya*, in the narrower sense of sexual restraint, was impracticable without *bramacharya* in the wider sense—the control in 'deed, word and thought' of all the senses. It was not a question of disciplining one appetite, but of all appetites; it was a rule of life, a weltan-schauung.

The connection between personal renunciation and service of mankind may not be obvious to most people, but men and women of God think otherwise. 'Somebody asked me', Mother Teresa, the Nobel Laureate saint of our time remarked, 'Are you married?' I said with a smile, 'Yes, to Jesus Christ'.[4]

The idea that the sublimation of sexual desire is a *sine qua non* for those who wish to attain a high spiritual state has been part of Hindu religious thought for centuries. It figures in the writings of all the great Indian saints, Jnaneshwar, Nanak, Kabir, Tukaram, Ramakrishna, Vivekananda, Ramana Maharshi and Muktananda.[5] It is accepted without demur by the common people as an ideal, which is realized but rarely. Most people in the West and Western-educated Indians, however, find it difficult to grasp this idea. Scholarly interpretations of Gandhi's concept of *brahmacharya* are usually in psychological terms, seeking its roots in his home influences and childhood experiences. 'Essentially, this [Gandhi's] attitude', Jawaharlal Nehru wrote in his autobiography, 'is that of an ascetic who has turned his back to this world and its ways . . . but it seems far-fetched to apply it to men and women of the world'.

Psychologists have tended to see Gandhi's attitude to sex as a peculiar personal phenomenon. His sexuality is seen as having been marred by, what to him was, 'juvenile excess', and charged with feelings of guilt. They also see certain extreme circumstances in Gandhi's life: 'his precocious sexual life, combined with his moral scruplosity', his aspirations, and gifts 'aided by the historical situation' which led him to a life of public service, and finally Kasturba's own extraordinary capacity for renunciation. Nevertheless, as the eminent Harvard psychologist Erikson reminds us, Gandhi's attitude made 'supreme sense', in the way he resolved his sexual conflicts, by making it 'a matter of will, sealed by a vow'.[6]

It is important to add that Gandhi's personality did not lose in tenderness, nor his attitude to women suffer from a perverted puritanism. Women, some of the most intelligent and noblest in India, were in his entourage, and in the vanguard of his movements. He became a champion of the political and social emancipation of women; his voice was raised against the tyranny of the *purdah* (the veil), the iniquity of child marriage, the ban on widow remarriage, and indeed against everything which cramped Indian womanhood. He roused India's women to a sense of their own dignity and power.

Of one thing there is no doubt. The transformation in Gandhi's life in South Africa, the snapping of the bonds of money, property and sex, and his conversion into, what Churchill was later to describe, as a 'naked faqir', enhanced Gandhi's capacity for single-minded devotion to public causes.

In an almost prophetic vein, Gilbert Murray had warned 'persons in power' in the *Hibbert Journal* in 1918 to be 'very careful how they deal with a man who cares nothing for sensual pleasure, nothing for riches, nothing for comfort or praise, or promotion, but is simply determined to do what he believes to be right. He is a dangerous and uncomfortable enemy because his body which you can always conquer gives you so little purchase upon his soul'.[7]

Gilbert Murray's warning was to be vindicated by the British dilemma in handling Gandhi during the following three decades. If the government found it impossible to bend or break the Mahatma, he was also immune to the erratic pressures of his own following. 'Those who claim to lead the masses', he wrote, 'must resolutely refuse to be led by them, if we want to avoid mob law and desire orderly progress for the country.' Gandhi was able to act on this principle because, as Lloyd and Susanne Rudolph point out, the 'serenity he achieved by his asceticism was . . . among his strongest assets as a leader of a mass movement that sometimes aroused strong feelings and evoked violent hatreds . . . . It lay at the root of his capacity to act sensibly in a crisis, to keep himself from being thrown off stride by other people's hysteria.'[8]

Finally, we come to the wild allegations in some of the more recent writings on Gandhi that during his Naokhali tour in East Bengal in 1948 'the Mahatma took young Hindu women to bed'. It is a grotesque distortion of the facts. During his stay in India, Erikson went into the details and put the story in perspective in his *Gandhi's Truth*.[9] In 1943, when Gandhi's wife was dying, she told her 74-year-old husband 'to take her place as a mother' to an orphaned young relative, Manu Gandhi. 'Gandhi took this role rather seriously', Erikson writes, 'being concerned, for example, with the girl's physical development . . . and having her sleep on a mat at the foot-end of his own mat and later, on occasions, "in his bed"—whatever that designation may mean in sleeping arrangements which included neither bedstead nor doors. The marked maternalism governing this relationship was later acknowledged in the very title of the young woman's memoir: "Bapu, My Mother".'[10] Erikson doubts whether there has ever been another political leader, who prided himself on being 'half man and half-woman . . . more motherly than women born to the job'. Commenting on Gandhi's 'public, private life', Erikson refers to an unusual quality in Gandhi, that of living and thinking aloud about inclinations which other men try to hide. Gandhi shared his passing thoughts and even embarrassing dreams with the readers of his weekly journals, thus making himself an easy target for malicious critics.

Erikson's judgement is confirmed by the considered opinion of N. K. Bose, the Indian anthropologist, Gandhi's secretary in 1946, who had initially raised this controversy. In an unpublished letter written in 1955,[11] Bose affirmed that there was no question of immorality on Gandhi's part, as he 'never slept in any room of his own. He used, generally, to sleep in the open verandah on a cot. Or even if he slept in a room, if there was no verandah in the house, there were others like Parsuram etc. (Gandhi's stenographer) who slept in beds beside him. Moreover, Gandhi tried to conquer the feeling of sex by consciously endeavouring to convert himself into a "mother" of those who were under his care, whether men or women'.

Bose refers to Gandhi's violent reaction against any physical manifestation of sex, and his psychological effort 'to become as pure as his mother', which led him into a 'profoundly significant attitude in public life'. Gandhi came to regard woman as the incarnation of *ahimsa* (non-violence).

> *Ahimsa* [Gandhi wrote] means infinite love, which again means infinite capacity for suffering. Who but woman the mother of man shows this capacity in the largest measure? She shows it as she carries the infant and feeds it during nine months and derives joy in the suffering involved. What can beat the suffering caused by the pangs of labour—who again suffers daily so that her babe may wax from day to day? Let her transfer that love to the whole of humanity. Let her forget she ever was or can be the object of man's lust. And she will occupy her proud position by the side of man as his mother, maker, and silent leader. It is given to her to teach the arts of peace to the warring world . . . [12]

Progress in civilization,[13] from this viewpoint, consisted in the introduction into human life and social institutions of a larger measure of 'the law of love or self-suffering', which woman represented best in her own person. 'This was', Bose writes, 'a profoundly transformed projection on the broad canvas of social life of an attitude which had come into being in the privacy of Gandhi's personal life'.[14]

CHAPTER 4

Gandhi and the Caste System

One of the charges levelled against Gandhi is that he acted as an apologist for the caste system, and in 1932, resorted to a fast 'to block an affirmative action' planned by the British government in favour of the outcastes, the so-called 'untouchables'. The fact is that no one did more than Gandhi to undermine the centuries-old caste system and to remove the blot of untouchability from Hinduism. The significance of his 1932 fast can best be appreciated in the historical perspective—the origins of the caste system, its uses and abuses, Gandhi's lifelong struggle against untouchability and the imperialist attempt in 1932 to turn a social problem of the Hindu community into a political weapon against Indian nationalism.

The origins of the caste system have been a matter of controversy among scholars, but it is generally accepted that its four main divisions were originally occupational, not essentially hereditary nor immutable. The system seems to have served a historic purpose. The Indo-Aryans, unlike the conquerors in some other continents, did not exterminate or enslave the indigenous populations. While maintaining their own superiority they sought to incorporate the original inhabitants in the social organization; thanks to the caste system, successive waves of invaders or immigrants from the north-west found a place within the Indian social fabric without losing their distinct identities. During periods of political upheavals, the caste system lent a certain resilience to the Hindu society, by providing a framework within which millions of people could live their lives irrespective óf what happened to the ruling dynasties and their clans. However, with the passage of time, the system came to acquire excessive rigidity; it became wholly hereditary, and was burdened with all kinds of taboos and notions of ceremonial purity which condemned those at the bottom of the social pyramid to petty tyranny and discrimination. Particularly hard was the lot of the 'outcastes', engaged in menial tasks ranging from scavenging to craftsmanship, which drew the compassionate advocacy of saints like Nanak, Kabir and Chaitanya in the mediaeval period, and of social reformers like M. G. Ranade and Jyotiba Phule in the nineteenth century. The forces of orthodoxy were, however, too deeply entrenched to be easily dislodged. It was left to Gandhi to shake Hinduism out of the centuries-old grooves of caste rigidity and the evil of untouchability.

II

Gandhi has narrated in his autobiography how he came face to face with untouchability in his home. His mother shared the caste prejudices which were common among Vaishnava Hindus. The children had orders not to defile themselves by touching the family sweeper Uka or by playing with 'untouchable' classmates. Gandhi was an obedient child, but he visibly chafed at these restraints; even at an early age, he sensed the inconsistency between the practice of untouchability and the beautiful anecdote of the epic *Ramayana*, in which he had heard of the hero Rama being ferried across the Ganges by a low-caste boatman. As he grew up, this fellow-feeling with the lowliest of the low grew. In South Africa, Gandhi's associates belonged to all classes and communities. To the first ashram at Ahmedabad, which he founded after his return to India in 1915, he welcomed an untouchable family; this action outraged the rich merchants of Ahmedabad, who were contributing to the upkeep of the ashram. Several associates deserted him in protest. Starved of funds, and with the few inmates at the ashram, who still stood by him, Gandhi thought of moving into the slums of Ahmedabad. An anonymous donor, however, rendered this course unnecessary.

During the first four years after his return from South Africa, while Gandhi was on the periphery of nationalist politics, he carried on ceaseless propaganda against the evils of untouchability. He even made this reform a plank in his political campaign in 1920–2. Untouchability was a recurrent theme in his speeches

during his country-wide tours in the twenties. At the Round
Table Conference in London in 1931, it hurt him to see the
representatives of the untouchables play into the hands of
reactionary, communal and political elements. He opposed the
segregation of the untouchables into a separate electoral group
as had been done in the case of Muslims, Sikhs and Christians.
How strongly he felt on this subject was revealed in a speech he
delivered at the meeting of the Minorities Committee on 13
November 1931:

> I claim myself in my own person to represent the vast mass of the
> untouchables. Here I speak not merely on behalf of the [Indian
> National] Congress, but I speak on my own behalf, and I claim
> that I would get, if there was a referendum of the untouchables,
> their vote and that I would top the poll. We do not want on our
> register and on our census 'untouchables' classified as a separate
> class. Sikhs may remain as such in perpetuity, so may Muslims, so
> may Europeans. Would untouchables remain untouchables in
> perpetuity?

In March 1932, while Gandhi was in jail, he wrote to Sir
Samuel Hoare, the Secretary of State for India on the 'Communal
Award', which the British government were to give on the
quantum and mode of representation in legislatures under the
new constitution. He told Hoare that separate electorates would
divide the Hindu community without doing any good to the
untouchables. He recalled what he had said at the London
conference, that he would resist with his life the grant of separate
electorates to the depressed classes. 'This was not said', Gandhi
wrote, 'in the heat of the moment or by way of rhetoric'.

When the Communal Award was published on 17 August
1932, it confirmed Gandhi's worst fears. In spite of the double
vote given to the 'depressed classes' (untouchables) for their
own separate constituencies as well for the general (Hindu)
constituencies, the fact remained that separate electorates were
to be set up for these classes. Gandhi immediately wrote to
Ramsay MacDonald, the British Premier, that he proposed to
undertake 'a perpetual fast unto death' which could only end, 'if
during its progress, the British Government, of its motion or
under pressure of public opinion, revised their decision, and
withdrew their scheme of communal (separate) electorates for
the depressed classes'. The fast was to continue even if he was

released. Three weeks later, Ramsay MacDonald acknowledged Gandhi's letter and defended the decision of the government as an effort to justly weigh conflicting claims. The British Premier and his advisers could not understand Gandhi's emotional and religious approach to the problem. They even scented a political motive in his fast; it seemed to them that Gandhi was trying a stunt to recover the prestige he had lost through the decline of civil disobedience.

If the British ministers failed to fathom the depth of Gandhi's feeling on this subject, they were even less able to see the ethics of fasting for the solution of, what was to them, a political problem. Fasting struck them as a thinly-disguised method of coercion. The British reaction to Gandhi's fasts was well exemplified in David Low's cartoon as a 'Prophecy for 1933' in which Lord Willingdon, the then Viceroy of India, was shown going on hunger strike at the instance of 10 Downing Street, 'to force Mr. Gandhi to admit the new constitution'.

Was fasting a form of coercion? Gandhi was aware that his fasts exercised a moral pressure, but the pressure was directed not against those who disagreed with him, but against those who loved him and believed in him; he sought to prick the conscience of the latter and to convey to them something of his own inner anguish at a monstrous social tyranny. He did not expect his critics to react in the same way as his friends and co-workers; if his self-crucifixion could demonstrate his sincerity to the teeming millions of India with whom he had identified himself, the battle would be more than half-won. E. Stanley Jones, the American missionary, asked Gandhi in Yeravda Jail: 'Isn't your fasting a species of coercion?' 'Yes,' Gandhi replied, 'the same kind of coercion which Jesus exercises upon you from the Cross'.[1] The fast dramatized the issue at stake; ostensibly it suppressed reason, but in fact it was designed to free reason from that mixture of inertia and prejudice which had permitted a gross social injustice to be tolerated by the Hindu society for centuries.

The news that Gandhi was about to fast shook India from one end to the other. 20 September 1932, when the fast began, was observed in the country as a day of fasting and prayer. At Santiniketan, the poet Rabindranath Tagore, dressed in black, spoke to a large gathering on the significance of the fast, and the

urgency of fighting an age-old evil. There was a spontaneous
upsurge of feeling; temples, wells and public places were thrown
open to the untouchables. A conference of the leaders of caste
Hindus and untouchables was convened at Poona to devise
alternative electoral arrangements to replace those provisions
of the British Communal Award which had provoked Gandhi
to offer the supreme sacrifice. An agreement was reached, and
none too soon. The alternative electoral arrangement for
depressed classes, which was hammered out at Gandhi's bedside,
provided that voters from the depressed classes would hold a
preliminary election and choose a panel of four candidates for
each seat; these candidates were to submit for election to a joint
election by caste Hindus and depressed classes. The number of
seats for depressed classes in provincial legislatures was raised
from 71 in the British Award to 148. Reservation of seats was to
continue until it was ended by mutual agreement. The new
electoral arrangement, which came to be known as the Poona
Pact, was accepted by the British government, and Gandhi
broke his fast on 26 September 1932 in the presence of
Rabindranath Tagore.

Gandhi was later criticized by some Hindu leaders, especially
in Bengal, for yielding too much to the depressed classes; but he
hated this constitutional arithmetic. He felt that, for all the
wrongs they had done to their weaker brethren in the past, caste
Hindus could never be too generous. The fast had at least one
good result; it did away with separate electorates for the
depressed classes. The insidious influence of this mode of representation as a wedge in Indian politics was to become fully
visible in the next decade. In 1909 the introduction of separate
electorates in the Minto-Morley scheme of reforms had created
an institutional base for the growth of Muslim separatism;
twenty-three years later, a similar attempt to make a mighty
hole in the nationalist front was foiled by Gandhi's fast. If the
Communal Award had not been amended by the Poona Pact in
1932, the solution of the Indian political problem during the
years 1945–7 would have become infinitely more difficult than
even it actually was.

During the negotiations for the transfer of power Ambedkar
staked out a claim that his Scheduled Caste Federation represented all the 'sixty million' scheduled castes and he was their

sole, authentic spokesman. He argued that the scheduled castes needed special safeguards and recognition as a minority such as had been accorded to the Muslim community; he almost spoke in Jinnah's idiom, denouncing 'caste Hindu domination'.[2] He called for separate electorates and even 'separate settlements' for scheduled castes. The British had a soft corner for Ambedkar. He had been a member of the Viceroy's Executive Council since 1942. Lord Wavell had included his name in the list for the Interim Government during the discussions at Simla Conference in 1945. The situation, however, changed after the general elections to provincial legislatures early in 1946. Ambedkar's party was routed by the Congress. It then became impossible for the government to recognize him as a spokesman of the scheduled castes. Ambedkar questioned the results of the 1946 election held under joint electorates; he railed against 'caste Hindu tyranny' and threatened 'direct action'.[3] He appealed to Prime Minister Attlee to intervene. Attlee was advised not to take any notice of Ambedkar's protests.[4]

If Gandhi had not fasted in 1932 and the separate electorates for scheduled castes in the Communal Award had not been modified by the Poona Pact, it is likely that the problem of scheduled castes would have added to the complexity of the negotiations in 1946–7, already bedevilled by Muslim separatism and princely intransigence.

More important than the constitutional arrangements—which incidentally did not come into operation for the next three years—was the emotional catharsis through which the Hindu community passed. The fast was intended, as Gandhi avowed, 'to sting the conscience of the Hindu community into right religious action'. The scrapping of the separate electorates for the depressed classes was to be the beginning of the end of untouchability.

One of the greatest campaigns of social reform in history was launched by a state prisoner. Gandhi issued a series of press statements and a stream of letters to his numerous correspondents to educate the people on the evil of untouchability. He arranged for the publication of a weekly paper, *Harijan*, to promote his campaign. 'Harijan' means 'children of God'; it was Gandhi's name for the outcastes, the untouchables. 'All the religions of the world [Gandhi wrote] describe God pre-eminently the friend of the friendless and help of the helpless, and the protector of the weak. Who can be more friendless, or helpless or weaker than the forty million or more Hindus of India, classified as untouchables?' Gandhi doubted whether there was any support for untouchability in the Hindu scriptures. But even if it were possible to cite a sanction for this tyranny from any ancient manuscript, Gandhi did not feel bound by it. Eternal truth, he asserted, could not be confined within the covers of a book, however sacred it might be. Every scripture had contained certain universal truths, but it also included injunctions relevant to the contemporary society; the latter, if they did violence to human dignity, could be ignored. A good chunk of the *Harijan* was written by Gandhi himself. He took the lead in pulling out the skeleton of untouchability from the Hindu cupboard and publishing graphic pen-pictures of the miserable condition in which the 'outcastes' lived.

After his release from jail, Gandhi embarked on a tour, which covered 12,500 miles, to purge Hinduism of the evil of untouchability. He pleaded with the Hindus to shed their prejudice against the Harijans; he urged the Harijans to shake off the vices—drugs and drink—which hindered their absorption into Hindu society. He ridiculed the superstition that anybody could be unclean by birth, or the shadow or touch of one human being could defile another. He wore himself out in making collections for the 'Harijan Fund'. In ten months, he received eight lakhs of rupees. He could have obtained this amount as a gift from a single Maharaja or a millionaire, but he did not set much store by money as such. The millions of men, women and children, who contributed to his begging bowl, became fellow-soldiers in the fight against untouchability.

The Harijan tour was by no means a triumphal progress. Gandhi was attacking an age-old tyranny and long-established vested interests which did not stick at anything to preserve themselves. The orthodox Hindus accused him of a dangerous heresy; they organized black-flag demonstrations; they heckled him, and tried to disrupt his meetings. On 25 June 1934, while he was on his way to the municipal hall in Poona, a bomb was thrown at his party; seven persons were injured, though Gandhi was unhurt. He expressed his deep pity for the unknown thrower of the bomb. 'I am not aching for martyrdom', he said, 'but if it came in my way in the prosecution of, what I consider to be, the supreme duty in defence of the faith I hold in common with millions of Hindus, I shall have well earned it'.

Even though the opposition of the orthodox Hindus died hard, and even though militant Harijan leaders were critical, Gandhi succeeded in piercing an ancient sore. Rajagopalachari, one of the front-rank nationalist leaders, in an article entitled, 'The Revolution is Over', wrote: 'What remains is but the removal of the debris'. This was an optimistic verdict, but there is no doubt that the reformists had made a good beginning. The Congress ministries in 1937–9 removed some of the legal disabilities of the Harijans, and untouchability itself became illegal in the constitution of the Indian Republic which came into force in 1952. A social tyranny, which had deep roots, needed a continuous war for many years on all fronts—legal, social and economic—but there is no doubt that Gandhi's campaign dealt it a heavy blow.

III

While Gandhi's opposition to untouchability was consistent and uncompromising, his attitude to the caste system—of which untouchability was a morbid growth—seemed to be marked by a certain ambivalence in the early years after his return from South Africa. The Hindu epics had given him a romantic image of the *varnashrama*, in ancient India, the fundamental four-fold division, in which castes were the equivalent of trade guilds, and birth was not the sole determinant of status and privilege. It seemed to Gandhi that the system, despite its obvious faults, had served as a cushion against external pressures during turbulent periods; he wondered whether it could be restored to its pristine purity and adapted to the changing needs of Hindu society. This was the background of some complimentary references he made to the caste system, which are often quoted against him. It must, however, be borne in mind that all the kind words he ever said about the caste system were about what he believed it to have been in the hoary past and not about what it was in his own time. Closer acquaintance with the Indian social scene convinced him that the system was so flawed by superstition, 'touch-me-not-ism', social inequality and discrimination, that it was past mending.

We can see a progressive hardening of Gandhi's attitude to the caste system. In December 1920, he wrote, 'I consider the four divisions alone to be fundamental, natural and essential. The innumerable sub-castes are sometimes a convenience, often a hindrance. The sooner there is fusion, the better'.[5] Fifteen years later he declared that 'the *varnashrama* of the *shastras* [scriptures] is to-day non-existent in practice. The present caste system is the very antithesis of *varnashrama*. The sooner public opinion abolishes it, the better'.[6] He suggested that all Hindus should voluntarily call themselves *shudras*, who were supposed to be the lowest in the social scale.[7] He rejected the notion that untouchability was an essential part of Hinduism; it was, he said, a 'plague which it is the bounden duty of every Hindu to combat'.[8] In the 1920s, he had been prepared to defend taboos on inter-dining and inter-marriage between members of different castes as exercises in self-restraint. In the 1930s, he was denouncing any exclusiveness which stemmed from caste or local prejudice. 'It must be left to the unfettered choice of the individual', he wrote, 'as to where he or she will marry or dine. . . .'[9] If India is one and indivisible, surely there should be no artificial divisions creating innumerable little groups, which would neither inter-dine nor inter-marry.'[10] In 1946, Gandhi made the startling announcement that no marriage would be celebrated in his ashram at Sevagram, unless one of the parties was an 'untouchable' by birth.

Gandhi's reluctance to make a frontal assault on the caste system in the early years may have been a matter of tactics. In a conversation with the Hungarian journalist, Tibor Mende, in 1956, Jawaharlal Nehru recalled:

> I spoke to Gandhi repeatedly: why don't you hit out at the caste system directly? He said that he did not believe in the caste system except in some idealized form of occupations and all that; but that the present caste system is thoroughly bad and must go. 'I am undermining it completely', he said, 'by my tackling untouchability'.
>
> You see . . . he had a way of seizing one thing and concentrating on it. 'If untouchability goes', he said, 'the caste system goes'.[11]

CHAPTER 5

The Fight Against Racialism

Gandhi was in South Africa for nearly twenty years between 1893 and 1914. These were the formative years of his life in which he developed ideas and methods which were to have a profound effect upon the history of India, and indeed of the world. Doubts have, however, been cast on Gandhi's South African record: it is argued that since he championed the cause of the Indian immigrants, and did not take up cudgels on behalf of the black population of Africa, he was not really against racialism.[1]

To appreciate the scope and significance of Gandhi's struggle in South Africa, it would be useful to briefly racapitulate the situation with which he was confronted. When he arrived in Natal in 1893 at the age of twenty-three, to serve as counsel of an Indian firm in a civil suit, he knew next to nothing about the 'Indian problem' in South Africa. This problem had its origins nearly thirty years earlier with the import of 'indentured' labourers from India to work sugar, tea and coffee plantations in Natal; their condition was, to use Sir W. W. Hunter's phrase, a 'condition of semi-slavery'. They had been recruited from some of the poorest and most congested districts of India; a free passage, board and lodging; a wage of ten shillings a month for the first year rising by one shilling every year, and the right to a free return passage to India after five years' indenture (or alternatively, the option to settle in the land of their adoption) had lured thousands of poor and illiterate Indians to distant Natal. By 1890 nearly forty thousand had been imported as indentured labourers. Not all the European employers were cruel, but it was difficult to change employers on the plea of ill-treatment, and if a labourer did not renew his 'indenture' after five years, he was hemmed in by all sorts of restrictions.

Nevertheless, many of these labourers, having lost their roots in India, preferred to settle in Natal. They bought small plots of land, grew vegetables, made a decent living and educated their children. This aroused the jealousy of the European traders, who began to agitate for the repatriation of every Indian labourer, who did not renew his indenture. In other words the Indian was wanted in Natal as a 'semi-slave', or not at all.

The Indian merchant followed the Indian labourer to South Africa and found a ready market among Indian labourers as well as the blacks. This naturally roused the opposition of the European trader; a law passed by the Natal legislature in 1894 was specially designed to disfranchise the two hundred-odd Indian merchants who had become entitled to vote. Indian trade and immigration were placed under galling restrictions; no one could trade in Natal without a licence, which a European could have for the asking, and an Indian could have only after much effort and expense, if at all. And since an educational test in a European language was made a *sine qua non* for entering the country, the door was barred and bolted against the majority of potential immigrants from India except, of course, the semi-slave 'indentured' labourers who continued to be imported.

The legal disabilities on Indians were bad enough, but the daily humiliations they suffered were worse. Every Indian without distinction was called a 'coolie'—a contemptuous word for a labourer. Indian school-masters were 'coolie school-masters', Indian store-keepers were 'coolie store-keepers', Gandhi was a 'coolie barrister'. Even the ships owned by Indians were called 'coolie ships'. Indians were commonly described as 'Asian dirt to be heartily cursed, chockful of vice, and he lives upon rice, and the black vermin'.[2] In the statute-book they were described as 'semi-barbarous Asiatics, or persons belonging to the uncivilized races of Asia'. They were not allowed to walk on the footpaths, or to be out at night, without a permit. First and second-class railway tickets were not issued to them; if a white passenger objected, they could be unceremoniously bundled out of a railway compartment, they had sometimes to travel on foot-boards of trains. European hotels would not admit them. In the Transvaal, they could not trade or reside except in specified locations, which the London *Times* described as 'ghettoes'. In the Orange Free State, there was a law prohibiting 'Asiatics and other coloured persons' from trading or carrying on any business whatsoever. 'Wherever the Indian goes', wrote the *Cape Times*, 'he is the same useful well-doing man, law-abiding under whatever form of government he may find himself, frugal in his wants and industrious in his habits. But these virtues make him a formidable competitor in the labour markets to which he resorts'.

The hostility of European politicians, officials and merchants, and the helplessness of the Indian merchants and labourers drew young Gandhi into the vortex of the politics of Natal. The Natal Indians had no franchise and no representation in the local legislature. Most of them had learnt to pocket their humiliations in a distant land as they pocketed their daily earnings. Socially and economically they were a heterogeneous group. It was no easy task for Gandhi to infuse a spirit of comradeship among the Muslim merchants and their Hindu and Parsi clients from western India, the semi-slave indentured labourers from Madras, and the Natal-born Indian Christians. The Boers and the Britons, whatever their differences, were united in their resolve to preserve the white monopoly of economic and political power. The Government of India, which had permitted emigration to the colonies in Africa, was not conversant with the true state of affairs, and the Colonial Office in London was reluctant to interfere in, what was described, as an 'internal affair' of self-governing colonies.

Gandhi was thus fighting against heavy odds. It was the hey-day of European imperialism; white domination over the coloured races—brown, black and yellow—was taken almost as a fact of nature. The Indians in South Africa, small in number, scattered in several colonies, hailing from various parts of India, ranging from a few rich merchants to thousands of poor semi-slave labourers, lived in constant dread of fresh restrictions and humiliations. Gandhi had to reckon with the unrelenting hostility of the European population and the colonial governments. In 1897 he was nearly lynched in the streets of Durban by a white mob. Eleven years later, in the course of the Satyagraha struggle, after he had reached an understanding with General Smuts, one of his countrymen nearly beat him to death for an alleged sellout of the Indian cause to the colonial government.

Gandhi had to evolve a strategy to suit the situation facing

him in South Africa. The colonial governments seemed imper-
vious to the appeals for justice. Gandhi sought the support of
Indian political leaders and British statesmen to restrain the
colonial regime from its headlong pursuit of racial discrimination.
He moderated his demands to elicit the widest sympathy. He
persevered in an unremitting public dialogue with the colonial
statesmen. He appealed to the reason and the conscience of the
saner section of the European community in South Africa. Even
after the transition from constitutional agitation to 'passive
resistance' or satyagraha, Gandhi did not adopt extreme
postures. He challenged the South African government on
specific and limited issues, such as repeal of the offensive
procedure for registering Asiatic immigrants, removal of
oppressive restrictions on Indian traders, and recognition of
marriages solemnized under the Hindu and Muslim laws.

In South Africa (as in India later) Gandhi put forward
modest demands even though they had long-term potentialities
for altering the status quo. Even in the last phase of his struggle
in South Africa, he did not fight for the redress of all the Indian
grievances; he confined himself to a few issues on which the
position of the government was demonstrably untenable. All
that he was able to achieve by 1914—when he left South
Africa—was to make the first dent on the armour of white
racialism. The more important demands of the Indian community such as the right to vote and to be represented in the
colonial legislatures had not even been advanced by Gandhi;
they were reserved for a later occasion.

The rulers of South Africa were shrewd enough to perceive
that Gandhi's fight on behalf of the Indian community had
profound implications for the racial issue in South Africa. This
indeed accounted for their tenacious opposition to the very
moderate demands of the Indian community under Gandhi's
leadership. As General Botha explained in a speech in 1913:

> . . . there was only one road to be followed in dealing with the Asian
> question . . . . He hoped people not living in South Africa would
> realise that their [the South African Government's] attitude in
> regard to the Asiatics was not prompted by a desire to get rid of the
> Asiatics, but was prompted by principle. In this country they had
> coloured races to deal with and they did not want to have the
> position complicated any further.[3]

If the black population did not figure in Gandhi's campaign it was partly because it did not suffer from the specific disabilities against which the Indians were protesting. The £ 3 tax on the Indian indentured labourers, the restrictions on immigration from India, and the legitimacy of Hindu and Muslim marriages under the Indian laws concerned only the Indian immigrants. In some ways, such as the eligibility for ownership of land, the natives of Africa were indeed better off than the Indians. Moreover, it seems doubtful whether at the turn of the century the black population in South Africa would have readily accepted a young Indian barrister as its leader. Leadership is not a cloak that one can put on at will. The position Gandhi came to acquire in the Indian immigrant community owed a great deal to a certain ethos; his personality, and methods were hardly likely to make an immediate appeal to the black population, or to other immigrant groups, such as the Chinese, in South Africa.

In retrospect, it seems that it was a sound instinct which guided the young Gandhi to wage his battle against racialism on a limited front. It was in South Africa that Gandhi acquired those remarkable qualities of leadership which enabled him to take the levers of the Indian nationalist movement in his hands. If he had clashed head-on with the Boer-British combine on the all-embracing issue of racial equality, he would have been bundled out of South Africa. In that event, the cause of racial equality would have suffered the most in the long run.

There is plenty of evidence to show that the emergent nations of Africa in their struggle for liberation from colonial rule received encouragement from Gandhi's example. African leaders have borne testimony to the inspiration they derived from Gandhi. 'Through the deliverance of India', Gandhi had written in 1921, 'I seek to deliver the so-called weaker races of the earth from the crushing heels of Western exploitation in which England is the greatest partner. India's coming to her own will mean every nation doing likewise'.[4] When Indian independence became a fact in 1947, it triggered—as Gandhi had predicted—the process of liquidation of colonialism and racialism in the whole of Asia and Africa.

It must be conceded that in South Africa, the scene of Gandhi's early struggles, the citadel of racialism has not yet fallen. But even in South Africa, Gandhi's example has been a source of inspiration to those who sought to resist the policies of racial discrimination. The South African National Native Congress (later renamed as the African National Congress) came into existence in 1912, just two years before Gandhi left South Africa; its constitution endorsed 'passive action' (i.e., passive resistance) as a means to be used for the redress of grievances.[5] Brutal repression by the police and aggression by the dominant white community may have been factors in frustrating the use of Gandhian techniques of resistance. However, a speaker at the African National Congress in 1930 pointed out, 'There is not a single man in South Africa who could make a success of passive resistance. You must have a leader who is prepared to make sacrifices such as Gandhi in India. We have no such leader'.[6] In 1946, the Indian Congress in Natal and in Transvaal, under a new and militant leadership, embarked on a 'passive resistance' campaign. Thousands of people joined the campaign and some of the younger African nationalists, such as Nelson Mandela, were especially enthusiastic about it. In 1949 and the early fifties, a programme embracing boycott, strikes and civil disobedience was adopted by the African National Congress. Three years later, there was a 'Defiance Campaign' in which Gandhi's son, Manilal, participated, and 8500 Africans and their allies went to gaol.[7] Chief Luthuli, the President-General of the African National Congress from 1952 to 1967, who received the Nobel Peace Prize, was profoundly influenced by Gandhi's teachings. He advocated non-violent resistance as a 'non-revolutionary, legitimate and humane' means to bring about partnership in the government of the country on the basis of equality.

Gandhi's ideas and methods were a strong formative influence in the history of African nationalism and Black militancy. The West African Congress was established in 1920; its founders were inspired by the example of the Indian National Congress. In the 1930s the course of the Indian nationalist struggle under Gandhi's leadership was being closely followed in other parts of the British empire. In the 1940s Kwame Nkrumah of the Gold Coast (later Ghana) was 'toying with Gandhi's ideas on non-violent campaigns and dreaming about translating them into action'.[8] In 1958, when the All-Africa People's Conference met in the newly independent state of Ghana, the Gandhian ideas were still relatively so popular in Africa that the Algerian National Liberation Front, engaged in a revolt against the French, had much difficulty in securing for their armed struggle legitimacy and support.

The most distinguished and enthusiastic exponent of Gandhi's ideas in Africa was Kenneth Kaunda of what was then Northern Rhodesia (now Zambia). 'Gandhi and Jesus', writes Kaunda's biographer, 'had a special magnetism for twenty-four-year old Kaunda. He saw them as realists with a vision and rejected the popular notion that this was a contradiction in terms.'[9] When Kaunda visited India in 1975, he recalled: 'Mahatma Gandhi and Pandit Nehru were heroes not only of the Indian people but of the entire oppressed peoples of the world. At least that is how we saw them in that part of the world'.[10]

It is true that since the 1960s Gandhism has declined in much of Africa, especially after the revolutionary struggles in Angola and Guinea Bissan under the influence of Marxism, but then this seems to be not only part of the world-wide escalation of tension and violence, but the result of the peculiar power-alignments and rivalries within and outside the continent of Africa.

There is no doubt that the movement for civil rights and racial equality in the United States of America was influenced by Gandhi's ideas of which Martin Luther King was an ardent champion. In his *Stride Toward Freedom* he tells us how he found in Gandhi's philosophy of non-violent resistance the satisfaction which he had missed 'in the utilitarianism of Bentham and Mill, the revolutionary methods of Marx and Lenin, the social contracts theory of Hobbes, the "back to nature" optimism of Rousseau and the superhuman philosophy of Nietzsche.'[11] Martin Luther King came to the conclusion that Gandhi's was 'the only morally and practically sound method open to oppressed people in their struggle for freedom'.

CHAPTER 6

Amritsar, 1919

The sequence of the Amritsar massacre of 1919 in the Gandhi film has been criticized as a 'misrepresentation' of what actually happened. The fact is that it is one of the very few episodes of which an authentic visual reconstruction was possible, because Jallianwala Bagh, the site of the tragedy at Amritsar, has been preserved as a 'memorial'.

In view of the enormous documentation available on the events of 1919, it seems incredible that efforts should be made to explain away General Dyer's crime. A British journalist has posed the question: 'When a lot of people get killed in a riot, who is most to blame, a clumsy commander like Dyer, or a consummate sorcerer's apprentice like Gandhi?'[1] The fact is that there was no riot in Amritsar on the day the massacre took place, and the events in that town had very little to do with Gandhi, who had never visited the Punjab, and whose name was not yet one to conjure with in that province.

The tradegy of Jallianwala Bagh hastened the process of Gandhi's alienation from the British Raj and dramatically altered the course of Indian politics. To see it in perspective, it is necessary to briefly recapitulate the events in Amritsar during the preceding week. On 6 April 1919, like many other towns in India, Amritsar witnessed a *hartal* (cessation of business) as a protest against the passage of the Rowlatt Bills, which had been enacted in the teeth of the unanimous opposition of *all* Indian members of the Imperial Legislative Council including those nominated by the government. Four days later, on 10 April, the arrest of two local leaders, Satya Pal and S. D. Kitchlew, triggered a melancholy chain of incidents. A crowd of mourners, bare-headed, bare-footed and unarmed, marched towards the residence of the British Deputy Commissioner to plead for the release of the two leaders. The procession was stopped and fired upon by a military picket. The crowd fell back, but it was no longer a peaceful crowd. The sight of the dead and the injured infuriated some hot-heads, who ran amuck, burnt down a post office, a bank and a suburban railway station, and killed four innocent Europeans. Order was restored by drafting troops into the town under Brigadier-General Dyer. For the next two days the city was quiet, and there was no untoward incident.

The thirteenth of April was the annual Baisakhi festival when Amritsar attracted peasants from surrounding villages for a visit to the Golden Temple in the morning, and for a little fun and shopping during the day. That afternoon, a public meeting was held at 4.30 p.m. in Jallianwala Bagh, an irregular square of waste land surrounded by houses on all sides. The attendance at this meeting has been variously estimated between 6000 and 20,000. General Dyer heard about this meeting and resolved to break it up. He took with him two armoured cars and 75 Gurkha and Baluchi troops. The entrance to the Jallianwala Bagh being too narrow to permit the armoured cars, Dyer marched in with fifty riflemen, and found himself on a raised ground overlooking a hollow field full of people. To his heated imagination it appeared to be an assembly of 'agitators', potential 'rebels'; in fact, it was a holiday crowd of peasants from surrounding villages and local residents, some of whom had infants in their arms. They were all hugely enjoying themselves, listening to a harangue from a speaker on a raised platform. Few of them knew that public meetings had been banned in the city by the orders of the military commander. It turned out later that notices imposing the ban had not been pasted on the walls of the city, and the town-criers, who had been sent to make the announcement with the beat of the drum, had done their job perfunctorily.

General Dyer deployed his fifty Gurkha and Baluchi soldiers along the whole length of the rising ground. What followed may best be narrated in his own words in answer to the questions from the Hunter Committee:

Q. When you got into the [Jallianwala] Bagh, what did you do?
A. I opened fire.
Q. At once?

A. Immediately. I had thought about the matter and don't imagine it took me more than 10 seconds to make up my mind what my duty was.

Q. ... On the assumption that there was ... risk of people being in the crowd who were not aware of the proclamation [banning all meetings in Amritsar], did it not occur to you that it was a proper measure to ask the crowd to disperse before you took that step of actually firing?

A. No, at the time I did not. I merely felt that my orders had not been obeyed, that Martial Law was flouted, and that it was my duty to fire immediately by rifle.

Q. Before you dispersed the crowd, had the crowd taken any action at all?

A. No Sir. They had run away, a few of them.

Q. Did they start to run away?

A. Yes. When I began to fire, the big mob in the centre [of the Bagh] began to run almost towards the right.

Q. Martial Law had not been proclaimed. Before you took that step which was a serious step, did you not consider as to the propriety of consulting the Deputy Commissioner, who was the civil authority responsible for the order of the city?

A. There was no Deputy Commissioner to consult at the time . . . . I considered it from the Military point of view that I ought to fire immediately.

Q. In firing, was it your object to disperse?

A. No, sir. I was going to fire until they dispersed.

Q. Did the crowd at once start to disperse as soon as you fired?

A. Immediately.

Q. Did you continue firing?

A. Yes.

Q. After the crowd indicated that it was going to disperse, why did you not stop?

A. I thought it was my duty to go on until it dispersed. If I fired a little, I should be wrong in firing at all.

Dyer stated that from time to time he 'checked his fire and directed it upon places where the crowd was the thickest'. The firing stopped when all the ammunition—1650 rounds—with his fifty riflemen had been expended. He admitted that he made no provision for aiding or removing the wounded; it was not his duty to render aid. 'That was', he said, 'a medical question'. As soon as the firing ceased, he retired with his soldiers.

The Punjab government estimated that 379 persons were

killed and 1200 injured. However, according to its own version, the government did not start investigating the figures of casualties until 24 August—four months after the tragedy. The Congress Enquiry Committee, which included some of the most eminent lawyers in India, Motilal Nehru, C. R. Das and M. R. Jayakar, and the report of which was drafted by Gandhi, estimated that 1200 lives were lost and three times as many were wounded.

The day after the massacre, Dyer addressed a meeting of prominent citizens in the local police station. He directed them to ensure that the shops, which had been closed as a protest against the firing, were reopened. 'Do you want war or peace?' he asked. 'For me the battlefield of France or Amritsar is the same. I am a military man and I will go straight. Neither shall I move to the right, nor to the left. Speak up, if you want war . . . . In case there is to be peace, my order is to open all shops at once . . . otherwise the shops will be opened by force and by rifles'.

Worse was to follow. On 15 April, martial law was clamped not only on Amritsar but on several other towns in the Punjab. It is not necessary to recount in detail this draconian regime which lasted for nearly two months. In Amritsar the most notorious order of General Dyer required Indians to crawl on their bellies in a street where a European woman had been assaulted. But almost everywhere the people were subjected to needless humiliations. Indians were made to alight from vehicles if a European passed on the road, and salute him, motor cars owned by them were requisitioned. In Lahore a thousand college students were made to march in the scorching heat of May four times daily, sixteen miles a day, to answer a roll call. When a notice pasted on the outer wall of a college building was found torn, every male in the precincts of the college, including the teachers, was arrested. The military officers, who committed these barbarities and heaped insults on the Indians, believed that they were holding the bastion of the British empire at a critical moment. Many of them had recently returned from European and Middle Eastern battlefields, and were impatient of half-hearted methods. Rabindranath Tagore, who renounced his knighthood as a protest against the events in the Punjab, rightly diagnosed the root of the trouble: 'What happened at Jallianwala Bagh was itself a monstrous progeny of a monstrous war'.

The Punjab government headed by Sir Michael O'Dwyer persuaded itself that there was a dangerous conspiracy to over-throw the Raj. When the Viceroy, Lord Chelmsford, advised Sir Michael to avoid dramatic punishments, his reply was that martial law could not be administered with kid gloves.[2] Sir Michael later claimed to have nipped the 'Punjab Rebellion' in the bud. The theory of a conspiracy was, however, not accepted even by the official intelligence agencies. When Robertson, Bombay's Inspector-General of Police, wrote to C. R. Cleveland, Director, Intelligence Bureau of the Government of India, enquiring if he had been able to trace any organized conspiracy, Cleveland's reply (23 May 1919) was: 'So far no traces of organized conspiracy have been found in the Punjab. There was organized agitation and then in particular places the people went mad'.[3]

General Dyer was not quite consistent in his defence in his successive explanations to General Beynon, his immediate superior, to the Hunter Committee, to the Army Council and to the press after his return to England. The plea that he was confused by cross-examination conducted by clever Indian lawyers is untenable; some of the statements which most damaged his case were made by him before the Hunter Committee and in reply to questions from its British members. Dyer admitted that he had ordered firing without warning and that he continued to fire for ten minutes even while the crowd was trying to disperse. He might have used machine-guns if he could have got them in. He also admitted that his force was not really in danger; he could have dispersed the mob without firing, but then they might have laughed at him and made him feel a fool. He had fired 'to teach them a lesson', to strike terror, to create a moral effect. And having exhausted his ammunition, he had marched away, leaving the wounded to take care of themselves.

Initially, there was much sympathy for Dyer in the army circles in India. The Adjutant General, Sir Havelock Hudson, defended his action in the Indian Legislative Assembly during the discussion on the Indemnity Bill. Dyer was even promoted to officiate as a Divisional Commander in a temporary vacancy. However, after his evidence before the Hunter Committee and the growing public criticism of the martial law regime in the

Punjab, it became impossible for the government to defend his action.

Curiously enough, it was not so much the brutality of Dyer and the rigour of the martial law regime in the Punjab, as the British reaction to them during the next twelve months which alienated Gandhi and nationalist India from the Raj. The first impulse of the Government of India was to defend the action of 'the men on the spot'. The Punjab was practically sealed from the rest of the country; even lawyers from the neighbouring provinces were not allowed to defend the accused being tried by martial law tribunals. The official enquiry committee, presided over by Lord Hunter, divided on racial lines; the three Indian members dissented from the majority report signed by their British colleagues. One of the Indian members, the eminent jurist and moderate politician, Sir C. H. Setalvad, tells in his memoirs, how in the course of a discussion, Lord Hunter lost his temper with him and exclaimed: 'You people want to drive the British out of the country'. After this, according to Setalvad, the Indian members and Lord Hunter, though under the same roof, almost ceased to speak to each other.[4]

The English-owned newspapers in India, with the exception of the *Times of India*, gave varying degrees of support to General Dyer, who was lionized as the 'Saviour of the Punjab'.

The majority report of the Hunter Committee signed by the European members held Dyer guilty on two counts: that he had fired without warning, and that he had gone on firing even after the crowd had begun to disperse. The Committee felt that Dyer's intention to create a moral effect was a mistaken conception of his duty. The Committee did not accept the view that by his action Dyer had saved the situation in the Punjab and avoided a rebellion on a scale similar to the Mutiny of 1857.

As the truth about the happenings in the Punjab came out, Edwin Montagu, the Secretary of State for India, who had been gallantly defending his subordinates in India, was shocked and embarrassed. He saw that the alienation of Indian opinion was likely to ruin the success of the constitutional reforms for which he had laboured for two years. He suggested the immediate suspension of Dyer, and enquired from the Viceroy whether Sir Michael O'Dwyer, the Lt. Governor of the Punjab, could be impugned for approval of Dyer's action. Another member of the

British Cabinet, Winston Churchill, who was Secretary of State for War, also took a serious view of Dyer's conduct. However, neither Montagu nor Churchill could have their way. The Viceroy did not favour drastic action against Dyer or the censuring of Sir Michael O'Dwyer, and the Army Council in England agreed only to the mildest possible action against Dyer who was retired on half pay with no prospect of future employment for committing 'an error of judgment'.

In the House of Commons, Churchill pooh-poohed the idea that Dyer had saved India. He said there were more British troops in India than at the time of the Mutiny, and they were 'supported by appliances' which did not exist in 1857: 'the aeroplanes, the railways, and wireless', which gave increased means of concentrating the troops where they were required.

Churchill criticized Dyer's declared intention to teach a moral lesson as 'terrorism, frightfulness', and referred to the Jallianwala Bagh tragedy as a 'monstrous event', that stood 'in singular and sinister isolation'. Some Labour M.P.s were even more emphatic in their denunciation of Dyer. Colonel Wedgwood said that it was the gravest blot on English history since the burning of Joan of Arc.

Unfortunately for the government, these words of Montagu, Churchill and Wedgwood were drowned in the din raised by the admirers of Dyer in England and India. In the House of Commons as many as 129 members voted against the government's motion censuring Dyer's action. Montagu was shouted down for encouraging lawlessness in India and asked to resign. A petition signed by 93 members of Parliament was presented to Prime Minister Lloyd George calling for Montagu's resignation from the Cabinet.[5] The Tory back-benchers were so angry with Montagu for his criticism of Dyer that some of them could have even physically assaulted him. In the House of Lords, the government suffered a defeat on this issue. The *Morning Post* set up a fund to support Dyer. In December 1920, Dyer received a cheque for £26317 with a letter from the editor of the *Morning Post*: 'Your conduct has met with the approval of a large number of your countrymen although no sums of money can possibly repay the debt the Empire owes you'.

Those who hailed Dyer as the 'saviour of India' were a vociferous minority in Britain; by their acclamation of Dyer

they were merely demonstrating their belief that a European
life was of greater value than an Indian's and that the British
had the divine right to rule the natives. This belief had been
buttressed by a century of Pax Britannica and confirmed by
Britain's victory in the First World War. As a British writer
puts it: 'The retired majors of Cheltenham and the blood-thirsty
spinsters of Pimlico were drunk with victory. Dyer became a
symbol of their belief in the overwhelming might and righteous-
ness of Britain'.[6]

Gandhi, who had spent three months in personally collecting
and sifting evidence for the enquiry committee appointed by the
Indian National Congress, was shocked by the obstinate refusal
of the government to make amends for the excesses committed in
the Punjab. What disturbed him and other nationalist leaders
was not so much the action of British officers in panic, but the
cold-blooded reaction of the British ruling class after the event.
The deep feeling aroused by the Punjab affair powerfully contributed to the anti-British feeling which fuelled the non-cooperation
movement. A letter written by Sir Valentine Chirol (of *The
Times*) who toured India at the end of 1920 summed up the
traumatic effect of the events in the Punjab even on moderate
Indian opinion: 'The conviction has been forced upon me that
the Punjab issue still dominates the whole situation & that the
intense bitterness has been produced by many of the methods of
repression, by the long delay in investigating the facts, by the
mildness of the ultimate official censure & penalties & by the
attitude of Parliament & the glorification of Dyer in certain
European circles at home and out here . . .'[7] The Duke of
Connaught, who visited India in February 1921 to inaugurate
the new central legislature set up under the Reforms Act of
1919, remarked: 'The shadow of Amritsar has lengthened over
the fair face of India'.

CHAPTER 7

The Two Faces of Imperialism

Is it fair, some critics of Gandhi ask, to judge the British record in India by an aberration, the massacre of Amritsar in 1919? That massacre was, we are told, 'not typical'; if British rule for a century had only one serious blot, it was not doing badly'.[1] It is further claimed that British rule in India was just and beneficial, inspired by the highest motives, and that 'the vast majority of those who served in the government of India were devoted to justice and welfare of the people'.

It is certainly true that terrorism and brutality did not form part of the normal methods of British administration in India. The East India Company was able to extend its rule over the Indian subcontinent, with a remarkable economy of British blood and treasure, by skilfully exploiting the weaknesses and rivalries of the Indian princes; it kept up the fiction of Mughal suzerainty for many years, and then gradually, almost imperceptibly, tightened its grip on the country. However, the rebellion of 1857 revealed that the British could be as vindictive and barbarous as any other conqueror, when their position was challenged.

When the British troops shelled their way back into Delhi in the autumn of 1857, the aftermath of the Mutiny was (in the words of a British historian) 'a case of the scorpians of Rehoboam following the whips of Solomon'.[2] No man's life was safe in the city; all able-bodied men were taken for rebels and shot at sight. Three Mughal princes were killed in cold blood by Captain Hodson; twenty-one more were hanged shortly afterwards. 'It is a great pity', wrote Sir John Lawrence, the Lt. Governor of the Punjab, about Bahadur Shah, the aged Mughal King of Delhi, who had been taken prisoner, that 'the old rascal was not shot directly he was seen'. As late as 12 December 1857, Sir

John was enquiring: 'Is private plundering still allowed? Do officers go about shooting natives?'[3] After the city had been ransacked and looted, the 'prize agents' of the victorious army were still busy, digging up the floors and walls of deserted houses in search of buried treasures. G. O. Trevelyan, the nephew and biographer of Macaulay, described, how after the capture of Delhi, 'every member of a class of religious enthusiasts named "Ghazis" was hung, as it were, ex-officio; and it is to be feared that a vindictive and an irresponsible judge, who plumed himself upon having a good eye for a "Ghazi", sent to the gallows more than one individual, whose guilt consisted in looking as if he belonged to a sect which, probably was hostile to our religion'.[4] There had been a massacre of European women and children at Cawnpore; it was amply avenged by General Neill's victorious army by the wholesale slaughter of the inhabitants of the town. According to Trevelyan, many people in England 'chuckled to hear how General Neill had forced high caste Brahmins to sweep up the blood of Europeans murdered at Cawnpore, and then strung them in a row without giving them the time requisite for purification'.[5]

The holocaust in the wake of the capture of Lucknow was no less indiscriminate. According to an eye-witness—a British army officer—'any unfortunate who fell into the hands of our troops was made short work of—sepoy or Oudh villager, it mattered not—no questions were asked; his skin was black, and did not that suffice? A piece of rope and the branch of a tree or a rifle bullet through his brain soon terminated the poor devil's existence'.[6]

The rebellion of 1857 was a reminder, if a reminder was needed, that the ultimate sanction for the rule of one country over another, was force. Henceforth the idea of 'division' and 'counterpoise' dominated British military policy in India. By 1863 the number of European troops was increased to 65,000; the Indian troops were reduced to 140,000 and came to be drawn from areas and communities whose loyalty had stood the test of 1857. The report of the commission on reorganization of the Indian army in 1879 mentioned the lessons taught by the Mutiny (which had) led to the maintenance of two 'great principles' of retaining in India an irresistible force of British troops and keeping the artillery in their hands. The main functions of the army were to be the protection of the frontier, and (what was euphemistically described as) 'internal security'.

Sir Henry Cotton, a member of the Indian Civil Service, who came out to India in 1867, wrote in his memoirs that the mutiny was then 'a living memory in the minds of all'.[7] Forty years later, Malcolm Darling, a young I.C.S. officer, fresh from England, noted in his diary that the memory of 1857 was like a 'phantom standing behind official chairs'.[8] The British in India remained prone to periodical attacks of 'mutiny-phobia'. In 1907 the Punjab government worked itself into a panic which proved to be wholly unjustified. The following year, in the wake of some terrorist outrages, there was a clamour for the imposition of martial law in Bengal. On such occasions, every Briton in India, from the Viceroy downwards, liked to think that he was defending an imperial outpost. 'The Raj will not disappear in India', Lord Minto, the Viceroy, wrote to John Morley, the Secretary of State for India, 'so long as the British race remains what it is, because we shall fight for the Raj as hard as we have ever fought, if it came to fighting, and we shall win as we have always won'.

Jawaharlal Nehru tells us in his autobiography about the panic which seized the European community in Allahabad when a number of Congress leaders, including Gandhi, visited Allahabad in May 1921 to attend the wedding of Jawaharlal's sister, Vijayalakshmi:

> I learnt one day through a barrister friend that many English people were thoroughly upset and expected some sudden upheaval in the city. They distrusted their Indian servants, and carried about revolvers in their pockets. It was even said privately that the Allahabad Fort was kept in readiness for the English colony to retire there in case of need . . . . It was said May 10th (the day accidentally fixed for my sister's marriage) was the anniversary of the outbreak of the mutiny at Meerut in 1857 and this was going to be celebrated![9]

In fairness to the British, it must be acknowledged that the more far-seeing among them recognized that they could do anything with bayonets, except sit on them. In 1899, Lord Elgin, the outgoing Viceroy, in an indiscreet outburst declared that 'India had been won by the sword and, if necessary, must be held by the sword'. He was soon corrected by Lord Curzon who had been designated to succeed him. 'The mission of the British', Curzon said, 'was to maintain with justice what has been won by the sword'.[10]

With no more than 1200 Britons in the I.C.S. and 700 in the cadre of the Indian Police, in a country peopled by 250 million, 'mass acquiescence' was a necessary buttress of the Raj. 'Empire', as a British historian reminds us, 'was impossible without Indian collaborators'.[11] The princes, the titled gentry, the landlords, the caste leaders, and some of the religious minorities were only too willing to play the part of collaborators. The majority of the members of the I.C.S. were hardworking and conscientious men, who were proud of their role in a system of paternalistic despotism. The district officer on horseback, touring the countryside, suppressing crime, dispensing impartial justice, visiting schools and dispensaries, was conscious of the awe and even the affection he inspired.

W. M. Thackeray, the novelist, wrote in 1844, that 'upon the whole a more humane, considerate and equitable government than that of the East India Company has seldom been witnessed in any country'.[12] Forty-two years later Sir Richard Temple, a former Governor of Bombay, was writing in a similar vein: 'In rectitude of purpose, in purity of motive, the Government of India cannot be surpassed'.[13] This habit of self-congratulation was part of the ethos of the British rulers of India. There were of course some who frankly viewed India 'as a distant station for troops, as a provision for the younger sons of Scottish Directors, as an investment of stock or as a last resource of aspiring lawyers and despairing maids'.[14] But Pax Brittanica was not wholly a British conceit; it was appreciated by the rising class of English-educated Indians. When Queen Victoria ascended the throne, they numbered a few thousand, and were largely confined to the presidencies of Bombay, Calcutta and Madras. When she died, they were half a million and found over the whole country. They believed that British rule had evolved order out of the political anarchy of the eighteenth century; that it had united the country, and linked it with a network of roads, railways, post offices and telegraph; that it had established a system of law and administration which recognized individual liberty, private property, freedom of thought and worship.

II

The response of the English-educated Indians to the Raj in the latter half of the nineteenth century could perhaps be best expressed in the words of M. G. Ranade, judge, historian, economist, educationist, social and religious reformer, who was one of the founding fathers of the Indian National Congress. The British nation, Ranade wrote, had its 'faults and foibles', but it had a moral element 'which inspires hope and confidence in colonies and dependencies of Great Britain, that whatever temporary perturbation may cloud their judgment, the reign of law will assert itself in the end'.[15] Ranade believed that under the impact of forces released by British rule, India had been roused from the stupor of ages, and there were forces at work which were assisting in her social, economic and political reconstruction. Western learning and science would liberate the Indian mind from the thraldom of old world ideas, and India would go forward along the road which England herself had traversed—that of constitutional and peaceful evolution. This interaction between the new and the old ideas, stimulated by contact with the West, was well summed up by Ranade's young friend and disciple, Gokhale:

> An ancient race had come in contact with another, possessing a more vigorous, if a somewhat more materialistic civilization, and if we did not want to be altogether submerged or overwhelmed, it was necessary for us to assimilate what was noble and what was vigorous in the new influences operating upon us, preserving at the same time what was good and noble in our own system.[16]

These tributes to Britain and her influence are the more remarkable because Ranade and Gokhale were men of the highest ability, integrity and courage of conviction. They were no favourites of the Raj. A high officer of the Bombay government had once described Ranade as the 'Hampden of the Deccan'.[17] Of Gokhale, Lord Hardinge, the Viceroy, wrote in 1912 that 'I mistrust him more almost than any man in India'.[18]

Admiration for the British did not, however, prevent Indian patriots from seeing the seamy side of imperialism. The inequitable allocation of the financial arrangements between Britain and India, and the fallacies in British economic and fiscal policies were exposed by Dadabhai Naoroji, Ranade,

Romesh Chunder Dutt and Gokhale. India was the biggest single foreign market for British exports, and the payments for 'home charges', the profits on British investments in India and Indian exports to hard currency areas provided 'the critical balancing item in the current balance of payments of the British Empire and more particularly of Britain with the rest of the world'.[19]

Apart from this economic and financial exploitation, there was perhaps no feature of British rule, which was more deeply resented than the virtual exclusion of the people of India from responsible positions in the civil and military services. No Indian could aspire to a higher rank in the army than that of a non-commissioned officer, a Subedar, who was junior to the freshest subaltern from England. Indians were permitted to sit for the entrance examination to the I.C.S. in London, but the dice were heavily loaded against them. They had to go to England to compete with the pick of English schools and colleges in subjects of study peculiarly English. To cap it all, the age limit was kept deliberately low; the candidates had to be below 19 years. The result was that the higher echelons of the administration were a virtual British monopoly. In 1897 Gokhale told the Welby Commission in London, that the result of this policy of discrimination was that 'we must live all the days of our life in an atmosphere of inferiority and the tallest of us must bend in order that the exigencies of the system must be satisfied. Our administrative and military talents must gradually disappear owing to sheer disuse, till at last our lot as hewers of wood and drawers of water in our country is stereotyped'.[20]

The I.C.S. included some remarkable Englishmen whose careers have been lovingly delineated by Philip Mason. But there is no doubt that the I.C.S. had grown into a close corporation of professional administrators who conducted themselves, and often really felt as if they were, in the words of W. S. Blunt, 'practical owners of India, irremovable, irresponsible and amenable to no authority than that of their fellow members'. They lived in a narrow, circumscribed world of their own—Anglo-India—which was neither England nor India. They claimed to be the trustees and guardians of the people of India, but they knew little about the common people and less about the rising educated class which aspired to a share in the governance of their country. Fleetwood Wilson, the Finance Member of Lord Hardinge's Executive Council, who did not belong to the I.C.S., noticed with the perceptive eye of an outsider, that the Anglo-Indian society in Simla and Calcutta was out of touch with the country over which it ruled:

> Extravagant, self-centred, artificial, it seemed blissfully unaware of the mountain of misery on which it sat; it was hardly conscious that the state revenue was wrung from a people who are perpetually on the borderland of starvation & who at the best of times have no luxuries & not much comfort.[21]

As the historian of the I.C.S. recognizes, however defensible the system may have been in the early years, India had outgrown it in the twentieth century. It was 'the despotism of a foreign caste'.[22] However benevolent it might try to be, it was a despotism all the same, 'as any system must be in which people are given what was good for them instead of what they want'.[23]

CHAPTER 8

The 1917 Declaration

Incredible as it may seem, Gandhi's contribution to the political liberation of India is being questioned. Paul Johnson, a British journalist, a former editor of the *New Statesman*, asserts that 'it is misleading to suggest that Gandhi was responsible for the British decision to leave India, that decision had already been taken before he began his campaign'.[1] Sir Algernon Rumbold, the author of a monograph on Indian politics during the years 1915–22, claims that 'it was not Gandhi's gimmicks which led to the British withdrawal, but the declaration of 20 August 1917 fore-shadowed the end of the British empire'.[2]

If the British government or its agents in India had decided to liquidate the Indian empire before the advent of Gandhi on the political stage, they were remarkably successful in keeping it a secret, for there is no evidence of such an intention even in their confidential records and correspondence.

In the last quarter of the nineteenth century, the leaders of Indian nationalism had looked forward to the day when their country would become a self-governing dominion within the British empire. A. O. Hume, a friend and confidant of Dadabhai Naoroji, W. C. Bonnerjee and Pherozeshah Mehta—whose role in the foundation of the Indian National Congress was crucial—expressed the hope in 1888 that 'fifty or seventy years hence . . . the Government of India will be precisely similar to that of the Dominion of Canada; when, as there, each province and presidency will have its local Parliament for provincial affairs, and the whole country will have its Dominion Parliament for national affairs, and when the only officials sent out to India from England would be the Viceroy and the Governor-General of India'.[3]

To the educated Indians who took an interest in politics, it was axiomatic that the road to Indian self-government lay through the gradual development of legislatures, with more elected members and larger powers. To British politicians and officials this seemed an impossible proposition. Lord Dufferin, during whose viceroyalty the Congress was founded, frankly doubted the feasibility of constitutional reforms in a conquered country 'in as much as self-government and submission to a foreign sovereign are incompatible terms'.

The stark truth was that at the turn of the century India was the linchpin of the commercial and defensive organization of the empire with which no ministry in Britain could dare to tinker. These were the days when imperialism was not a dirty word, and British statesmen could speak frankly about what Britain gained from the Indian connection. Lord Curzon, speaking in 1909 as an ex-Viceroy at Edinburgh, asserted that India was not merely a 'magnificent jewelled pendant, hanging from the Imperial collar, capable of being detached there from without making any particular difference to its symmetry or strength', but 'the strategic centre of imperial defence, the granary of Britain, the source of plantation labour for the colonies, and of raw materials for the home industries, and an outlet for British capital and manufactures and a training ground for young Britons in the arts of peace and war'.[4]

It was only natural that the talk of constitutional reforms and self-government should have disconcerted the British rulers. George Hamilton, the Secretary of State for India, was of the opinion that the principle of racial equality between Europeans and Indians should never have found a mention in Queen Victoria's Proclamation of 1858. The introduction of the English legal system, literary education, competitive examinations and a free press in India—all these seemed to him in retrospect a series of blunders.

The agitation against the Ilbert Bill in the early 1880s had revealed the width of the gulf between the ruling race and the people of India. An attempt by Lord Ripon's government to rectify some anomalies in the trial of Europeans by Indian judges, nearly provoked a 'white mutiny'. Seton-Kerr, a former Foreign Secretary to the Government of India, declared that the Ilbert Bill outraged the 'cherished conviction which was shared by every Englishman in India from the highest to the lowest, by the planter's assistant in his lowly bungalow, and the editor in the full light of the presidency towns—from these to the Chief Commissioner in charge of an important province and to the Viceroy on his throne—the conviction in every man that he belongs to a race whom God had destined to govern and subdue'.[5]

The British officials questioned the fitness of the Indian people for self-governing institutions. But in fairness to them it must be conceded that some of them were not sure that the British parliamentary system was worth emulating. James-Fitzjames Stephen, a former Law Member of the Government of India, argued in his book, *Liberty, Equality, Fraternity*, that the English parliamentary system paralyzed executive government, and was a hindrance to good government even in his homeland.[6]

Most British officials disputed the right of the rising class of educated Indians to speak for the masses. They saw no need to appease this class, which was in any case a 'microscopic minority'. 'The real guarantees of our stay in India', Lord Lamington, the Governor of Bombay, wrote, 'remain as strong as ever viz., the caste system, the diversity of nationalities and creeds and the lack of confidence and trust of one native for another'.[7] 'We must realize', B. Fuller, a former member of the I.C.S. and a retired Governor, wrote in 1910, 'that we are foreigners in this country and a foreign government in the nature of things cannot command much popular sympathy'.[8] R. H. Craddock, the Chief Commissioner of the Central Provinces, later, the Home Member of the Government of India, wanted to put a stop to all talk of parliamentary government for India. 'There was no question of India being on a par with British Dominions at any time', he wrote, 'the National Congress must either drop its colonial [Dominion] swaraj creed or cease to exist . . . . How long are we to listen to this nonsense about swaraj on the colonial system, which is an impossible ideal? . . . Any toying with these people is toying with criminals and rebels'.[9]

It is not surprising that the Morley–Minto Reforms of 1909 fell far short of the hopes of Indian nationalists. John Morley, the Liberal Secretary of State for India, ruled out parliamentary institutions for India. He was assured by the Viceroy, Lord Minto, that what galled the educated Indian was not the humiliation of foreign subjection, but the frustration of personal ambition; a judicious distribution of more and better-paid jobs could, therefore, turn malcontents into loyal adherents![10] The British bureaucrats in Simla and London used all their skill to concede as little as possible, and to hedge, what was conceded, with safeguards for the Raj. The elections to the 'reformed' legislatures were indirect, except in the case of the Muslims and the landlords. Of the twenty-seven elected members of the Imperial Legislative Councils, thirteen were elected by non-official members of the provincial legislative councils, six by Muslims and two by Chambers of Commerce. The franchise was narrow. For example, only eight electors chose the Muslim representative from Bombay.

The reforms were the handiwork of a Liberal government, but they belied the hopes of the most moderate of Indian nationalists. The truth was that neither the leadership nor the rank and file of the British Liberal Party were prepared for a radical change in India. Soon after taking office in 1905 the Liberal Prime Minister, Sir Henry Campbell-Bannerman, had declared: 'It has been a pretty unbroken rule, a wise rule that we assuredly shall not be the first to break, to keep questions of the internal administration of India outside the arena of party politics'.[11] The fact was that the attitude of the Liberal and Conservative parties towards India did not really differ in fundamentals. They were all for strong and impartial government, for justice between Indian and Indian and even between Indian and Briton. The Liberals were perhaps more willing than the Conservatives to agree to the widening of the base of the legislatures or to the appointment of Indians to a few high executive posts, but their object was not to transfer power to Indian hands but merely to provide safety-valves for political discontent. To a generation, which bitterly disputed the Irish claim that Ireland was a nation, self-government for India could hardly make sense.

Both Morley and Minto disclaimed any intention of launching India on the path to parliamentary democracy. Their successors—Lords Crewe and Hardinge—were equally emphatic that India must always remain a British dependency. Crewe, who succeeded Morley at the India Office, in a speech in the House of Lords in 1912 ridiculed the school of political thought in India which dreamt of dominion self-government: 'I say quite frankly, that I see no future for India on those lines. I do not believe, that the experiment of attempting to confer a measure of real self-government, with practical freedom from [British] parliamentary control upon a race which is not our own . . . is one which could be tried'.[12] In the same year, in a confidential minute circulated to the members of his executive council, the Viceroy, Lord Hardinge, wrote:

> Whatever may be the future political development of India, colonial self-government on the lines of British Dominions is absolutely out of the question. We have undertaken the serious and difficult task of guiding the destinies of India and of developing her civilization. Our task is not yet half-completed; and having put our hands to the plough, we cannot turn back. The pace has been quite fast enough of late—it would be wicked to accelerate it at the present moment.[13]

To Hardinge, a non-official majority in his legislative council was inconceivable. 'Once we have a non-official majority in the Viceroy's Legislative Council', he wrote, 'the Viceroy had better pack up his traps and leave the country. His position would be lacking in dignity'.[14]

Hardinge and Crewe echoed the thoughts not only of the British policy-makers in London and Simla, but of the whole of Anglo-India. The proposal to appoint Sir S. P. Sinha, an Indian, to the Viceroy's Executive Council (which Morley initiated, with Minto's concurrence) met with fierce opposition. Every member of the Viceroy's Executive Council, except one, was against it. The provincial governments were unanimous in their disapproval. The English-owned press in India was highly critical. In London, the Secretary of State's own Council was up in arms, and former Viceroys, Curzon, Lansdowne, Elgin and even Ripon, shook their heads. The Prince of Wales was scandalized, and King George V put on record his vehement protest against the decision of the Cabinet which was 'fraught with the greatest danger to the maintenance of the Indian Empire under British rule'.[15]

Neither the British government nor the Government of India had any intention of making a further move after the Minto-Morley reforms. But the outbreak of the First World War created a new situation; the economic and political ferment generated by the war could not be ignored. The Home Rule

Movement launched in 1916 by Tilak and Mrs Besant made a swift and strong impression on the country. Mrs Besant set up a branch of her Home Rule League in England. The comment of *The Times* was characteristic:

> We have received copies of a leaflet . . . by an obscure agency calling itself 'Home Rule for India League', which appears to have opened offices in London. The most ominous feature is concisely in the declaration that 'the Government of India must cease to be foreign and must become Indian'. A movement of this kind need not perhaps be taken seriously. Cranky people in this country do many mad things, but surely the maddest is to encourage a Home Rule agitation in India.[16]

The Home Member of the Government of India, Sir Reginald Craddock, who was responsible for law and order in the country, described Mrs Besant as 'a vain old lady influenced by a passionate desire to be a leader of movements'. Before long the government's reaction changed from derision to bewilderment, and from bewilderment to alarm. The objective of the Home Rulers, self-government for India within the British empire, may seem modest today, but in 1916 it alarmed the authorities. The movement deeply stirred the Western-educated classes and students; in some provinces it affected the countryside. 'Sedition in India', Craddock warned, 'is like the tides which erode a coastline as the sea encroaches . . . . We must have our dam in order lest it inundate sound land'.

The projected dam against the seditious flood was a declaration of British policy towards India. In a series of 'Clear-the-Line' telegrams the Viceroy, Lord Chelmsford, urged the Secretary of State, Sir Austen Chamberlain, to hasten an announcement by His Majesty's Government on post-war constitutional and administrative changes in India, so as to win over 'the influential, though timid, unorganized and comparatively inarticulate body of opinion which is opposed to and afraid of any sudden and violent changes in the constitution'. That the Viceroy did not envisage any radical changes in the immediate future was clear from his telegram of 11 June 1917: 'It seems to me that once we undertake to define our goal, we can say nothing but that it is the development of free institutions with a view to ultimate self-government. If such a declaration is made, then I think it should be accompanied by a very clear declaration that this is a distant goal and that anyone who pretends that it is realizable today or in the early future is no friend to Government and no friend to India herself . Clearly the Viceroy and his advisers wanted a statement which would have a soothing effect on Indian opinion, without committing the government to any substantial constitutional or administrative changes in the near future.

The British Cabinet was too preoccupied with the conduct of the war to spare much time for the niceties of the constitutional arrangements in India. Lloyd George, the Prime Minister, asked Curzon, a member of the War Cabinet and an ex-Viceroy, to take a hand in drafting the declaration of British policy the terms of which were being telegraphically discussed by the Government of India and the Secretary of State. Curzon's antipathy to Indian nationalism was known, but none of the British ministers was thinking in terms of a radical change in India. On 14 August 1917, when the matter was discussed by the Cabinet, Curzon explained his objections to the word 'self-government', because Indians would expect it to happen within a generation, 'while the Cabinet probably contemplated an intervening period which might extend to 500 years'. He, therefore, put forward his alternative formula about 'the full realization of responsible government'.[17]

Six days later, Edwin Montagu, who had recently succeeded Austen Chamberlain, as Secretary of State for India, read the long-awaited declaration in the House of Commons 'that the policy of His Majesty's Government in India was that of increasing association of Indians in every branch of the administration, and gradual development of self-governing institutions with a view to the progressive realization of responsible government in India as an integral part of the British Empire'.

The declaration was enthusiastically received in India. If it raised hopes of the establishment of a Westminster style democracy in India, it was not the fault of those who had drafted it, and certainly not of Curzon, who had approved it. It has been suggested that with all his vaunted mastery of the English language, Curzon may have meant 'responsible government' to mean only 'government by responsible men', and not 'an executive responsible to the legislature'. 'For once', writes

Curzon's biographer, 'his power of setting forth in precise
language exactly what he had in mind seems to have deserted
him.'[18]

Peter Robb, the historian of Chelmsford's viceroyalty, says
that the responsible government promised in 1917 meant 'in
fact the devolution of self-government upon the provinces but
under an enduring British Central Government: neither full
freedom nor a single Indian Dominion was envisaged. No
official had the courage to envisage complete [British] withdrawal, and later attempts were to be made to repudiate or
re-interpret these decisions'.[19]

Edwin Montagu summed up the British dilemma when he
recorded in his diary on 10 November 1917 that he was racking
his 'brains as to how I am going to get something which India
will accept and the House of Commons will allow me to do
without whittling it down'.[20]

Historians may differ on the exact date on which the British
decided to liquidate their Indian empire, but it certainly was
not in 1917, nor indeed, at any time before Gandhi assumed the
leadership of the Indian nationalist movement.

CHAPTER 9

Gandhi and the Raj

Lord Curzon, who had taken a hand in drafting the declaration of 1917, thought it would take India five hundred years to qualify for self-government. In 1906 Dadabhai Naoroji, the most venerated Indian politician of the day, exhorted Indian nationalists to persevere in the face of difficulties. 'The Irish have been struggling for 800 years', he wrote, 'and here they are struggling all the same!' A few years later S. P. Sinha, a brilliant lawyer and the first Indian member of the Viceroy's Executive Council, estimated that India would become a dominion in three hundred years.

The emergence of Gandhi on the political stage in 1919 upset all these calculations of British statesmen and Indian leaders. He remained the dominant factor in Indian politics for the next three decades; his confrontation with imperialism was to culminate in its liquidation not only in India but in the rest of the world. The final result was, however, obvious neither to the British nor to the Indians, while the struggle lasted.

Gandhi's emergence as the leading actor on the political stage was a phenomenon which was as bewildering to the Indian political elite of the day as it was to the British authorities.[1] He had returned to India early in 1915 after twenty years' absence in South Africa. For the first few years he seemed to be on the periphery of nationalist politics, strangely out of tune with the leaders of the day. At the annual sessions of the Indian National Congress, he was invited to speak on the problems of Indians overseas, but he was not in the inner group which shaped Congress policy. In 1917 he struck Edwin Montagu, the Secretary of State for India, as 'a social reformer with a real desire to find grievances and to cure them, not for any reasons of self-advertisement, but to improve the conditions of his fellow-

men. He dresses like a coolie, forswears all personal advancement, lives practically on the air and is a pure visionary'.

This image of a starry-eyed idealist was strengthened by
Gandhi's studied abstention from the Home Rule Movement
on the plea that it was wrong to embarrass Britain while she was
engaged in a life-and-death struggle during the World War. His
broadsides against the materialistic civilization of the West and
the use of English as a medium of instruction in Indian schools
grated on the ears of the Indian educated classes, who had
learnt to admire English literature, English history and English
politics. 'We have been engaged during the last sixty years',
Gandhi said, 'in memorizing strange words and their pronun-
ciation instead of assimilating facts'.

In the Indian National Congress Gandhi found himself out of
sympathy with both the Moderate and Extremist factions.
What dismayed him was their virtual insulation from rural
India, where 90 per cent of the population lived. Both the
parties shared the belief that the game of politics could best be
played in town-halls and council chambers by the educated,
especially the Western-educated, classes. What really divided
Gandhi from parties and politicians in the homeland was his
South African experience. Among the discoveries he had made
in the course of those twenty-odd years was that constitutional
politics for a subject people had definite limits. He realized that
a political contest was a conflict not merely of arguments, but of
interests, that a stage could be reached when something more
than reasoning was required to redress injustice and to shake off
oppression. In South Africa he had evolved his method of
satyagraha, of non-violent resistance as an alternative to the use
of force. It was as the author and practitioner of this method
that he was to come into a head-on collision with the British
Raj.

During the First World War, both Gandhi and the Government of India seemed to be consciously trying to avoid a confrontation. Hardinge had taken a hand, at the instance of
Gokhale, in resolving the deadlock between Gandhi and Smuts
in the final phase of the South African struggle. High British
officials in the Government of India seemed to be aware that
Gandhi was not a man to be trifled with. They took pains to
answer his letters and, when necessary, to explain things to him

in person. They hoped that his reforming zeal would drain off in
the innocuous channels of religious and social reform. Some of
them may even have hoped to enlist him as an ally, if he cast in
his lot with the Moderates. But they soon discovered that he
was much too independent, candid and unpredictable for their
taste. He seemed to them capable of conjuring a crisis out of
nowhere. He could draw the masses like a magnet, he could
make high dignitaries look foolish. Even while he criticized the
acts of British officials, he claimed to be their friend. After his
arrival in Champaran district in Bihar in 1917 had triggered a
first class agrarian crisis between the European indigo planters
and their Indian tenants, Gandhi wrote to the local magistrate
that

> my mission is totally of peace. The government machinery is
> designedly slow. It moves along the line of least resistance.
> Reformers like myself who have no other axe to grind, but that of
> reform they are handling for the time being, specialise and create a
> force which the Government must reckon with.

The Government of India went some way towards placating
Gandhi on the crisis in Champaran, and on such non-contro-
versial subjects as the emigration of indentured labour to the
British colonies. But they did not accept his claim that he was a
disinterested bridge-builder between the people and an irresponsible executive. They did not like his intervention on behalf
of the Ali Brothers, who had been interned for their Pan-Islamist
sympathies, or on behalf of the drought-stricken peasants in
Gujarat, who were pleading for a remission of land revenue.
The attitude of the Government of India towards Gandhi
hardened when he denounced the Rowlatt Bills. Lord
Chelmsford's reaction to Gandhi's call for satyagraha was to
'call his bluff'. The government thought of clapping him into
prison. On 11 April 1919 Sir George Lloyd, the Governor of
Bombay, met the Viceroy at Kalka near Simla to discuss a
proposal to deport Gandhi along with five other political leaders
to Burma. An idea of the official hostility to Gandhi may be
formed from a telegram sent by Sir William Vincent, the Home
Member, to the Moderate leader Surendranath Banerjee on 13
April in which he described Gandhi as having 'put himself
entirely beyond the pale. No one disputes Mr. Gandhi's sincerity

and we all regret his wrong-headedness, but I think you will agree he has crossed the boundary . . . . It is quite impossible to treat with him'.[2] Three days earlier, on 10 April, Gandhi had in fact been arrested while he was on his way to Delhi and brought back by train to Bombay. The disturbances in Bombay, Ahmedabad and other places provoked by his arrest, however, forced the government to retrace their steps. Gandhi himself was taken aback by the popular reaction to his arrest in his home province and helped in restoring peace quickly. Meanwhile, a terrible tragedy had been enacted at Amritsar and martial law proclaimed in the Punjab. Lord Chelmsford's government had burnt its fingers in the initial stage of Gandhi's Rowlatt Bills Satyagraha; if in the ensuing months it was reluctant to lay its hands on Gandhi, it was not because it had discovered the virtues of 'non-intervention', but because the risks of intervention seemed too great.

II

While launching satyagraha in 1919 Gandhi posed the issue between him and the authorities: 'The Government want to show that they can disregard public opinion. We must show that they cannot do so'.[3] During the next twelve months, other popular grievances, such as the attitude of the government to the Punjab tragedy and the Turkish peace treaty, were added to the Rowlatt laws. By the end of 1920 it was a straight fight for 'swaraj' (self-government) for India. Gandhi called for 'swaraj within a year'; constitutional reforms doled out in instalments were no longer acceptable. This demand seemed wholly unrealistic to the British rulers of India. The declaration of 1917 had never been intended as a promise of self-government in the near future; at best it was a will-o'-the wisp to beguile Indian nationalists for decades, if not for centuries. In February 1922, when Gandhi was planning a campaign of mass civil disobedience, Lord Reading, the Viceroy, was pulled up by his superiors in London for vacillation and weakness in handling the movement. We learn from the British Cabinet papers that Winston Churchill expressed his 'strong opposition to the prevalent idea that the British Raj was doomed', and insisted that Britain 'must strengthen her position in India'.[4] Lloyd

George, the British Premier, assured his colleagues that if there was an attempt to challenge the British position in India, 'the whole strength of Britain would be put forward to maintain British ascendancy in India. Every section of the population of Great Britain shared that view: a challenge to our position and rule in India would be taken up by the whole country with a strength and resolution that would amaze the world'.[5]

Lloyd George headed a coalition government. The Conservatives and the Liberals did not, however, differ on the essentials of the Indian policy. Nor did the Labour government during its brief tenure in 1924 show the will, or even the desire, to strike out a new line in its Indian policy. In 1929, when the Labour Party was voted back to office, the Viceroy, Lord Irwin, with the approval of Wedgwood Benn, the Secretary of State for India, issued a statement that 'the natural issue of India's constitutional progress', as contemplated in the Montagu's declaration of August 1917, was 'the attainment of dominion status'. The statement raised a storm in England. All the 'experts' on India including former Viceroys and Secretaries of State—Reading, Birkenhead, Peel, Winterton, Simon, Austen Chamberlain and Crewe—were scandalized by the specific reference to Dominion Status for India. The Labour government was on the defensive, and explained away the Viceroy's declaration as merely a re-statement of what had been said earlier. It is significant that the Simon Commission, in its report published in 1930, fought shy of the phrase 'Dominion Status', and never once used it.

The Labour government's brief experiment in political conciliation in 1930–1, which received a temporary boost from the Gandhi-Irwin Pact in 1931, came to an abrupt end with the onset of an economic crisis in Britain, and the formation of a Conservative-dominated 'National government' in the autumn of 1931. The British policy 'veered from the way of experimenting with partnership towards the old imperial ways of paternalism, collaboration and repression'.[6]

Since British public opinion was not ready for a real devolution of authority to Indian hands, it was necessary—as the *Manchester Guardian* once put it—to 'devise a constitution that seems like self-government in India and at Westminster like British Raj'. The architects of the Act of 1935 seized on the concept of an

All-India Federation, incorporating British Indian provinces and princely states, to weaken the nationalist element in the new constitution. As Sir Samuel Hoare, who piloted the reforms through the House of Commons, confided to his Conservative colleagues, the federal structure could be a handy instrument to yield 'a semblance of responsible government and yet retain in our hands the realities and verities of British control'.[7] Four years after the passage of the Act of 1935, the Viceroy, Linlithgow (who had been the Chairman of the Joint Select Committee of the British Parliament for constitutional reforms), reminded Zetland, the Secretary of State for India:

> After all we framed the constitution, as it stands in the Act of 1935, because we thought that was the best way—given the political position in both countries—of maintaining British influence in India. It is no part of our policy, I take it, to expedite the constitutional changes for their own sake, or gratuitously to hurry the handing over of controls to Indian hands at any faster pace than we regard as best calculated on a long view to hold India to the Empire.[8]

It was Linlithgow who, with Churchill's backing, spiked the guns of Sir Stafford Cripps, when he came out to India in April 1942. The following year, he told his successor Field Marshal Wavell that British rule in India would last for another thirty years.[9] As for Churchill, almost till the end, he remained the relentless opponent of Gandhi and Indian nationalism. We have it on good authority that he hoped for a solution of the Indian problem whereby the 'British might sit on top of a tripos-Pakhistan, Princely India and the Hindus'.[10] If he had been returned to power in 1945, it is not unlikely that he would have stalled a solution indefinitely, or attempted the balkanization of India so as to ensure Britain's position as the supreme arbiter in the subcontinent.

The British policy towards India thus grew out of the fundamental fact that there was an unbridgeable gap between what the British were prepared to offer and what nationalist India, led by Gandhi, was prepared to accept. It was only natural for the British to try to rally all those who were bound to them by the ties of self-interest—the princes, the landlords, the titled gentry, the religious minorities. It was also inevitable that when

Gandhi launched civil disobedience in 1919–22, 1930–1 or in 1940–2, the government used all its resources for the repression of the movement.

III

It has been suggested that Gandhi and the Indian National Congress were fortunate in being pitted against the British, 'a civilized and humane nation'. However, as the mutiny of 1857 had shown, when their power was challenged, the British could also be ruthless. There was no equivalent of Siberia in the Indian subcontinent, but hundreds of young men accused of terrorist conspiracies were deported to the far-off, dreaded islands, the Andamans. The British were careful not to repeat the Amritsar massacre of 1919, but when it came to repressing sedition, they were not held back by any 'misplaced' humanity. If the government took its time in arresting Gandhi in 1922[11] or in 1930, it was because it was uncertain of the popular reaction. The timing and the quantum of force used against the satyagraha struggles were intended to ensure the most favourable results from the official point of view. Lord Irwin did not interfere with Gandhi's march to Dandi for the breach of the Salt Laws, because the very idea of unseating the King-Emperor by boiling sea-water in a kettle was considered absurd and impractical. When the movement gathered momentum, the 'Christian Viceroy' struck hard, and issued a series of drastic ordinances to arm the executive with vast powers to suppress the movement; Congress processions and meetings were forcibly broken up, and more than 60,000 men and women were clapped into prison.

The Gandhi film includes a scene of the barbarous beating-up of Gandhi's adherents by the police at Dharsana Salt Works in 1930. The authenticity of this scene has been questioned by some critics, but it was actually witnessed by an American correspondent, Webb Miller of the *New York Telegram*, who recalled:

> In eighteen years of reporting in twenty-two countries during which I have witnessed innumerable civil disturbances, riots, street-fights and rebellions, I have never witnessed such harrowing scenes as at Dharsana. The Western mind can grasp violence

returned by violence, can understand a fight, but it is, I find, perplexed and baffled by the sight of men advancing coldly and deliberately and submitting to beatings without defence. Sometimes the scenes were so painful, I had to turn away momentarily. One surprising feature was the discipline of the volunteers. It seemed they were thoroughly imbued with Gandhi's non-violent creed . . . . During the morning I saw hundreds of blows inflicted by the police, but not a single blow returned by the volunteers.[12]

The Dharsana raid was not an isolated episode. William L. Shirer, a well-known journalist and author of *The Rise and Fall of Adolf Hitler*, who covered the Salt Satyagraha for the *Chicago Tribune* in 1930 has borne testimony to police beatings in Bombay, Calcutta, Delhi, Lahore and other places. 'It was a sickening sight', he writes in his memoirs. 'I had marvelled, at the magnificent discipline of non-violence which the genius of Gandhi had taught them. They had not struck back, they had not even defended themselves, except to try to shield their faces and heads from lathi blows'.[13]

Willingdon, who succeeded Irwin as Viceroy, had even fewer qualms in sanctioning sledge-hammer tactics against Gandhi and the Congress when he goaded them into a resumption of civil disobedience in 1932. The mood of the authorities in India is reflected in a letter written by Sir Frederick Sykes, the Governor of Bombay, to the Viceroy in November 1931, in which he urged 'a really rapid, organized and weighty handling' of civil disobedience. Sir Frederick wrote:

The last thing I can conceive, is that we should be justified in going slow until the movement gained strength. Above all, we must select our weapons to fight the Congress, and not fall into the mistake of doing what our opponents expect. I cannot do better than quote the views which the Commissioner of Police, Bombay, has recently expressed on the subject: 'They [the Congress] rely on the traditional humanity of the British combined with their fear of international criticism to protect them from any really drastic action, and they thus persuade us to fight this rebellion on their terms, and with methods chosen by them. We cannot possibly embark on another campaign of this kind of warfare. It prolongs the agony, and is undignified. Instead of fear, which is the root of all decent government, it begets contempt. It is in my opinion essential that the fact that the Government intends to treat a renewal of civil disobedience movement with the severity which a rebellion demands should be clearly demonstrated.'

The opinion expressed by some writers that the British deliberately handled Gandhi and the Congress softly has no basis
in fact. The repression unleashed by Willingdon early in 1932
was all-embracing. Through a series of ordinances the central
and provincial governments assumed every conceivable power.
The Congress Working Committee, the Provincial Committees
and innumerable local committees were declared illegal;
hundreds of organizations allied with or sympathetic to the
Congress, such as Youth Leagues, national schools, Congress
libraries and even Congress hospitals were outlawed. Buildings,
property, automobiles, bank accounts were seized; public
gatherings and processions were forbidden, and newspaper and
printing presses were fully controlled. Meetings were forcibly
dispersed. Punitive police was posted in refractory villages at
the cost of the inhabitants. Lands and houses seized for non-
payment of taxes were sold irrevocably for a song. Jail administration hardened. Gandhi's English discipline, Miss Slade,
the daughter of an Admiral of the British Fleet, gave an eye-
witness account of the conditions in a women's prison in
Bombay. Her neighbours in this gaol were three criminals, two
thieves and a prostitute; these criminals were not locked up for
the night, while the political prisoners were. Women political
prisoners were allowed to interview their children only through
iron bars.[14]

The government systematically choked the publicity channels
of the Congress. In the first six months of 1932, according to a
statement in the British Parliament, securities had been
demanded from 98 printing presses and action taken under the
Press Laws against 109 journalists.[15] In Bengal even the proceedings of the provincial legislative council could not be published if they contained criticism of the government. In some
provinces it was an offence for a newspaper to publish photo-
graphs of Gandhi and other Congress leaders. The Government
of India went so far as to seek the assistance of the authorities in
London to stop the royalties to the All-India Spinners' Association from the sale of Columbia Gramophone Company's record
containing a talk by Gandhi on the existence of God.

Those who want to get a feel of this period would do well to
read Jawaharlal Nehru's autobiography. He gives a glimpse of
the 'terrible occurrences' in Bengal and North-West Frontier

Province where the conditions resembled martial law, of the ordinances, of the hunger strikes and other sufferings in prison.

> Scores of thousands were refusing to bend before the physical might of a proud empire, and preferred to see their bodies crushed, their homes broken, their dear ones suffer, rather than yield their souls . . . . In our country, we move about as suspects, shadowed and watched, our words recorded lest they infringe the all-pervading law of sedition, our correspondence opened, the possibility of some executive prohibition or arrest always facing us.

In April 1932, Nehru's old mother Swarup Rani, the widow of the great Motilal Nehru, joined a Congress procession in Allahabad, which was stopped and beaten up by the police. She was knocked down and hit repeatedly on the head.

The British officials in India may have taken even harsher measures for the suppression of Gandhi's movements, but for two constraints under which they had to function. One was the fear of criticism in the British press and Parliament, which always had a few doughty champions of freedom for India. The other constraint was the fact that Gandhi's campaigns by and large remained non-violent, and barbarous treatment of men and women who had consciously renounced violence was likely to alienate even those who stood outside the political arena.

IV

Gandhi had his own constraints. Satyagraha required the severest self-discipline, the practice of non-co-operation with the opponent without hatred, and of resistance without retaliation. The adherent of satyagraha could invite suffering at the hands of the oppressor, but not inflict it on him. Gandhi deliberately discouraged the involvement of the peasantry and the industrial workers in his campaigns; he also excluded the princely states from the purview of his movement. All these self-denying ordinances were intended for better regulation of the movement and keeping it free from violence. In April 1919 while he was launching his first satyagraha struggle, Gandhi told C. R. Das, the nationalist leader of Bengal, that 'in Satyagraha there was no danger from outside, but only from within; if there was departure from truth and non-violence, whatever the provocation, the movement would be damned. Satyagraha admits of no compromise with itself'.[16] He advised Das to avoid processions and large gatherings until it was certain that the crowds could be controlled. When violence broke out at Ahmedabad and Bombay in the wake of his arrest in April 1919, he immediately suspended satyagraha. Three years later, in February 1922, he brushed aside the protests of his close colleagues, and called off mass civil disobedience after a riot in a remote village in the United Provinces, because he came to the conclusion that the atmosphere in the country was not favourable for a non-violent mass movement.

Some of Gandhi's colleagues chafed under the moral strait-jacket of satyagraha. It seemed to them that he expected too high a standard of conduct from a mass movement, that if all his instructions were fully observed the movement would be reduced to pious futility. Their scepticism was mirrored in a letter written in the early thirties to Jawaharlal Nehru by Rafi Ahmed Kidwai, a staunch Congress leader from the U.P. 'If we want to make further progress, we will have to make an attempt to destroy the mentality created by the C.D. [civil disobedience].... We will have to give up the present standards of scrupulousness, personal integrity, honesty and political amiability'.[17]

Ironically, Gandhi got no credit from the British for the restraints he imposed on his followers. The British rulers of India tended to see in Gandhi only a Machiavellian politician, with the Congress as his pliant tool, who was exploiting men and situations for his own ends. The political problem in India struck them primarily as an administrative one, requiring timely and judicious use of force. They could hardly see the intellectual and ethical roots of the movement for political liberation: the enthusiasm it evoked struck them as a variant of ignorant fanaticism. To Gandhi the non-violent basis of the movement was its most significant feature; to the British the conscious moral superiority of Gandhi and his followers was simply an additional irritation. As Willingdon put it in a speech to the Central Legislative Assembly on 5 September 1932: 'The leaders of the Congress believe in what is generally known as direct action, which is an example of the application of force to the problems of politics. The fact that the force applied is as a rule not physical force in no way alters the essential characteristics of the attitude which at the present moment inspires Congress policy'.

Those who had grown grey in the service of the Indian empire were not taken in by the language of non-violence, however much it was flavoured with morality and religion. They did not like the idea of being evicted from India even non-violently. And in fairness to them, it must be conceded that many of them sincerely believed that India, with its welter of races and languages and internal divisions and defencelessness against foreign invasion, was not ripe for self-government.

The guardians of the Raj had thus entrenched themselves behind a wall of prejudice. Gandhi's satyagraha struggles were designed to penetrate this wall. When reasoning failed, voluntary suffering at the hands of the opponent might melt his heart and release the springs which hindered understanding. In practice this method of 'attack' on the opponent was neither easy nor quick in producing results. Gandhi found that there was a limit to the number of patriots who could be persuaded to plunge in the non-violent fight for freedom, and open themselves to the risks of broken limbs, broken homes and broken careers. Those who took up satyagraha were enjoined to do their duty, irrespective of the chances of success or failure. There were, however, melancholy periods—such as during the years 1933–4 and 1943–4—when it was difficult to stem despondency and demoralization in nationalist ranks.

During his South African struggle and his visits to England in the years before the First World War, Gandhi had formed his own image of the British character. 'The British are said to love liberty for themselves and for others', he said, 'but they have a faculty for self-delusion that no other nation has'.[18] The British had, however, a quality, which Gandhi greatly admired. 'I have found Englishmen', he wrote, 'amenable to reason and persuasion, and as they always wish to appear just, it is easier to shame them than others into doing the right thing'.[19]

The confrontation between Gandhi and the British lasted for a quarter of a century. Gandhi's civil disobedience campaigns were a source of great anxiety and tension to the British authorities, while they lasted. But each campaign seemed to peter out after some time when the torrent of satyagrahi prisoners became a trickle. After each campaign, the government felt it had won a

victory over the Congress and Gandhi was finished as a political
leader. This was a delusion. In 1934 Willingdon was shocked,
when the Congress, despite the ruthless repression of the preceding two years, swept the polls in the election to the Central
Legislative Assembly. Linlithgow's ostensibly successful blitz-
krieg against Gandhi and the Congress in 1942 similarly proved
a Pyrrhic victory: the British had to pay heavily for it in the total
liquidation of the Raj.

V

In retrospect it seems that the ding-dong battle between Gandhi
and the government had results the significance of which was
not recognized at the time. Gandhi removed the spell of fear and
thus knocked off an important pillar of imperialism. He stemmed
the tide of political terrorism[20] which, starting from Bengal after
the partition of that province, had been rising throughout the
years of the First World War. During the next quarter century
in which the Congress was engaged in a fight with the government, it was able to throw up a cadre of political leaders capable
of taking over the reins of the government after the British
departure.

Gandhi's method created a dilemma for the British. If the
nationalist upsurge in India had been violent, the problem
would have been relatively simple. As it was, they found that
neither indifference, nor repression really worked against
Gandhi. Non-intervention allowed the agitation to snowball;
repression of unarmed men and women, who refused to retaliate,
won the sympathy of the multitude and deepened its alienation
from the Raj. The imperial base for collaboration was eroded
over the years. The princes, the landlords and the titled gentry
lost their influence and were of little use in bolstering the
prestige of the Raj. As the tensions between the political parties
sharpened communal antagonism and economic discontent
and increased turbulence in the towns and the countryside, the
thousand-odd British civil servants in India found the task of
governing the country unmanageable.

The Second World War changed the map of the world. The
United States of America and the Soviet Union emerged as the
two super powers, and Britain was left with neither the means

nor the will for a global, strategic and imperial role. The intellectual and social ferment in Britain, of which the Labour
Party's triumph in 1945 was an expression, helped in reassessing
the merits of traditional British policies towards India. Ideo-
logically, the Labour Party had been moving towards a new
orientation for quite some time; as far back as June 1938, Attlee
and Cripps had discussed with Jawaharlal Nehru possibilities
of early independence for India and of participation of the
Indian National Congress in the Government of India.[21] But
the facts of the Indian situation after the Second World War
also drove the Labour Party in the same direction. Speaking on
6 March 1947 in the House of Commons on the condition of
India in November and December 1945, A. V. Alexander, who
had been a member of the Cabinet Mission to India, recalled:
'It might be said that the Indian authorities were literally
sitting on the top of a volcano, and as a result of the situation
which had arisen after the war, the out-break of revolution
might be expected at any time'. Such was the irascibility of the
popular temper that early in 1946 there were violent outbreaks
at the slightest provocation, and sometimes without any provocation. There were incidents of indiscipline in the Air Force and
a major naval mutiny in Bombay. In several provinces there
were signs of disaffection spreading to the police. The instruments of law and order, on which the British rule ultimately
depended, were proving broken reeds.

It was, however, not merely the compulsion of events, but a
measure of idealism which inspired the policy which Prime
Minister Attlee initiated and carried through during the years
1946–7. And in so far as the British government was impelled by
this idealism, by a desire to open a fresh chapter in Indo-British
relations, it was a victory for Gandhi, who had pleaded for
nearly thirty years for a transformation of the relationship
between the two countries.

Malcolm Muggeridge, who spent a year in Calcutta in the
mid-thirties as Assistant Editor of the Calcutta *Statesman*, writes
in his memoirs that he could not recall meeting 'a single British
businessman or official, soldier or even missionary, who considered it possible that the British Empire in India was to end
before the twentieth century had half run its course'. The
British belief was that 'the Raj, in one form or another would go

on for centuries yet'.[22] Ten years later, when the Labour government decided to transfer power to Indian hands, many British politicians, officials and non-officials regarded it nothing short of a scuttle.[23] Their feelings are graphically reflected by the novelist John Masters, who came of a family that had served in India for five generations: 'Glamourous Dickie [Mountbatten] and Attlee with their three months' knowledge between them, breaking up in half a year what it took us centuries to build'. The despair and rage of the 'colonials', unable to reconcile themselves to decolonization in 1947, comes out in the words of John Masters' hero Rodney Savage: 'But it's time to go. That's the whole sad story. Time to go. But I'm not going. Never, see? It is not your country. It is mine. I made it for a hundred centuries. I and my great grand-father . . .'

It is doubtful, if without 'Gandhi's gimmicks'[24]—to borrow Sir Algernon Rumbold's phrase—the British would have wound up the Indian empire in 1947. The British historian Arnold Toynbee has therefore a point when he says that Gandhi was as much a benefactor of Britain as of his own country: 'He made it impossible for the British to go on ruling India, but at the same time he made it possible for us to abdicate without rancour and without dishonour . . . . In helping the British to extricate themselves from this [imperial] entanglement Gandhi did them a signal service for it is easier to acquire an empire than to disengage from one'.[25]

As Gandhi had hoped and predicted, the liberation of India in 1947 turned out to be a prelude to the liquidation of imperialism in Asia and Africa. In this process of voluntary decolonization and transmutation of their all-white empire into a multi-racial Commonwealth the British were guided by a sound political instinct. As Queen Elizabeth in her speech at Philadelphia on 6 July 1976 on the occasion of the United States Bicentennial said, 'the British lost the American colonies in the eighteenth century because we lacked that statesmanship to know the right time, and manner of yielding what is impossible to keep'.[26]

CHAPTER 10

Religion and Politics

'Mr. Gandhi's religious and moral views are, I believe admirable and indeed are on a remarkably high altitude', wrote Reading, soon after his first meeting with the Mahatma, 'but I must confess that I find it difficult to understand his practice of them in politics.'[1] Reading was not the only Viceroy in feeling the difficulty; his predecessors and successors had the same complaint. Indeed, some of Gandhi's own colleagues and followers grumbled that he tended to mix religion with politics.

Much of the confusion arose from the fact that Gandhi's concept of religion had little in common with what commonly passes for organized religion: dogmas, rituals, superstition and bigotry. Shorn of these accretions, Gandhi's religion was simply an ethical framework for the conduct of daily life.

Many people, who are prepared to concede the value of an ethical framework in domestic and social spheres, question its feasibility in politics, which are proverbially 'the art of the possible'. For most politicians politics is a game which they must play, and play to win; what is expedient takes precedence over what is moral. Tilak, the most influential nationalist leader in India at the time, told Gandhi in 1918: 'Politics are not for *sadhus* (holy men)'.[2]

Curiously enough, it was Gokhale, the Moderate leader, whom Gandhi hailed as his 'political mentor', who first talked of 'spiritualising politics'. Gokhale was far from being a man of religion; not even his worst enemies questioned his secular credentials. But his commitment to the nationalist cause was total, and his personal life was noted for its simplicity and austerity. He was convinced that India's dire need was of men who could give all their talents and all their time to her service. For centuries, India had her bands of *sanyasins* (ascetics) who had turned their backs upon worldly ambitions, and consecrated themselves to the service of God and man. Gokhale wondered whether this reserve of self-sacrifice could be tapped for the social and political regeneration of the country. In his farewell address to Fergusson College in 1904 he had said that 'the principal moral interest of this institution is in the fact that it represents an idea and embodies an ideal. The idea is that Indians of the present day can bind themselves together, and putting aside all thoughts of worldly interest, work for a secular purpose with the zeal and enthusiasm which we generally find in the sphere of religion alone'.[3]

This idea of 'spiritualising politics', of evoking abnegation and self-denial for secular causes, which inspired Gokhale to establish the Servants of India Society, also appealed to Gandhi; he applied it to the various ashrams he set up in South Africa and India. But he went further, and extended the application of this idea to the political field. Satyagraha, his method of resolving conflicts, drew its dynamic from his deeply-held religious and philosophical beliefs, which were not exclusively Hindu. He acknowledged his debt not only to the *Gita* and the *Upanishads*, but to 'the Sermon on the Mount', and the writings of Tolstoy and Thoreau. One can be an atheist or agnostic, and still practise satyagraha. But it is easier for men of religion to accept the assumptions on which satyagraha rests: that it is worthwhile fighting, and even dying, for causes which transcend one's personal interests, that the body perishes, but the soul lives, that no oppressor can crush the imperishable spirit of man, that every human being, however wicked he may appear to be, has a hidden nobility, a 'divine spark' which can be 'ignited'.

For Gandhi satyagraha was a way of life, but to many of those in the Congress Party, whom he led, it was just a method for waging the battle against the Raj. This divergence of approach between Gandhi and his following came out at critical junctures. In February 1922, when he decided not to proceed with mass civil disobedience after receiving the news of the Chauri Chaura riot, many of his colleagues protested that his emphasis on non-violence was overdone. In March 1931, his decision to call off civil disobedience and to attend a Round Table Conference in London came as a shock to his radical colleagues, especially to Jawaharlal Nehru. 'There comes a stage', Gandhi said, 'when a Satyagrahi may no longer refuse to negotiate with his opponents. His object is always to convert his opponent by love'. This talk of converting the enemy through love ruffled the 'realists' in his party; satyagraha seemed to have ethical and religious overtones which grated on their ears.

Gandhi's use of such words as 'swaraj' (self-government), 'sarvodaya' (uplift of all), 'ahimsa' (non-violence) and 'satyagraha' was exploited by the Muslim League to estrange Muslims from the nationalist struggle. The fact is that these expressions when used by Gandhi had little religious significance. They were derived from Sanskrit, but since most of the Indian languages are derived from Sanskrit, this made them more easily intelligible to the masses. The English translation of these words, or a purely legal or constitutional terminology, may have sounded more 'modern' and 'secular', but it would have passed over the heads of all but a tiny urbanized English-educated minority.

The protagonists of Pakistan made much play with the phrase 'Ram Rajya' which Gandhi occasionally employed to describe the goal of the Indian freedom struggle. This was Gandhi's equivalent for the English term 'utopia'. Gandhi was employing (what Professor Morris-Jones has aptly described) the 'saintly idiom'; the masses whom he addressed instinctively knew that he was not referring to the monarchial form of government described in the ancient epic *Ramayana*, but to an ideal polity, free from inequality, injustice and exploitation.

It is a remarkable fact that Gandhi adapted traditional ideas and symbols to modern needs, and transformed them in the process. He transmuted the centuries-old idea of an ashram as a haven from worldly life for pursuit of personal salvation: his ashrams at Sabarmati, and Sevagram were not merely places for spiritual seeking, but offered training in social service, rural uplift, elementary education, removal of untouchability and the practice of non-violence.

Prayer meetings have been a part of the daily life of the people in India from times immemorial; Hindus, Muslims and Sikhs daily gather in their temples, mosques and gurdwaras. These congregations are, however, sectarian affairs. Gandhi turned his prayer meetings, which were held not in a temple, but under the open sky, into a symbol of religious harmony by including recitations from Hindu, Muslim, Christian, Parsi and Buddhist texts. When the prayers and hymns had been recited, he spoke on the problems which faced the country. In the last months of his life, at a time of bitter religious controversy, his prayer meetings became a defiant symbol of tolerance, and his post-prayer talk served the purpose of a daily press conference.

Thus the symbols used by Gandhi in his political campaigns had ceased to be exclusively Hindu symbols. The 'saintly idiom' remained, but its content had changed; this is something which often escaped the attention of Gandhi's critics. One of them, M. N. Roy, who in his communist as well as Radical Humanist phases, had been sharply critical of Gandhi's 'religious approach to politics', confessed later that he had failed to detect the secular approach of the Mahatma beneath the religious terminology and that essentially Gandhi's message had been 'moral, humanist, cosmopolitan'.[4]

Deeply religious as he was, Gandhi said that he would have opposed any proposal for a state religion, even if the whole population of India had professed the same religion. He looked upon religion as a 'personal matter'. He told a missionary who asked whether there would be complete religious freedom in independent India, 'The State would look after your secular welfare, health, communications, foreign relations, currency and so on, but not your or my religion. That is everybody's personal concern.'[5] The resolution on fundamental rights, which the Karachi session of the Indian National Congress passed in 1931, with Gandhi's cordial approval, avowed the principle of religious freedom and adequate protection for minorities; it declared that the 'State shall observe neutrality in regard to all religions.' This doctrine was embodied in the constitution of independent India even after the Muslim League waged and won the campaign for the partition of the country on the basis of religion. Louis Fischer noted the strange paradox that Jinnah, who had grown up as a secular nationalist in his younger days, and who apparently had little interest in religion, founded a state based on religion, while Gandhi, wholly religious, worked to establish a secular state.[6]

Those who charged Gandhi with importing religion into politics pointed to his fasts as an example of this aberration.

They questioned the ethics of fasting as a political tactic. Were Gandhi's fasts not a form of moral coercion? Did they not detract from rational discussion of complex issues? C. F. Andrews, the Christian missionary, who was a friend of both Gandhi and Tagore, once wrote to the Mahatma from England: 'I hardly think you realize how very strong here is the moral repulsion against fasting unto death. I confess as a Christian I should do it, and it is only with the greatest difficulty that I find myself able to justify it under any circumstances'.[7]

Even though fasting had a place in the religious life of the Hindus for centuries, Gandhi's genius lay in creatively using it as a tool for social action. He described fasting as the 'most potent of the weapons' in his armoury of satyagraha. But he also described it as 'a fiery weapon', to be used sparingly, and as a last resort, when all other avenues of redress had been closed. However, he took care to use it against those who admired and loved him, never against his opponents. He did not, for example, fast to compel the Muslim League to give up its demand for Pakistan. He fasted to awaken the conscience of the Hindu community against untouchability, and to bring rioting mobs back to sanity.

We learn from Jawaharlal Nehru's autobiography that his first reaction to Gandhi's fast in jail in September 1932 was one of anger at his 'religious and sentimental approach to a political question'. And yet, a few days later, when there was an upsurge in the country against untouchability, Nehru could not help feeling 'what a magician . . . was this little man sitting in Yervada Prison and how well he knew to pull the strings that move people's hearts'.[8]

Of Gandhi's capacity to pull strings in the human heart, the greatest examples were to come in the last months of his life in the wake of the communal disturbances which preceded and followed the partition of the country.

CHAPTER 11

Gandhi and the Partition of India

John Vincent, Reader in Modern History at Bristol University, holds Gandhi responsible for the 'shedding of innocent blood during the massacres', which occurred in the aftermath of the partition of India in 1947. He calls this the 'climax of Gandhi's life' and adds: 'The British foresaw this danger; Gandhi did not, or shut his eyes to it . . . . Better the stuffiest of British officers, I would say than a skilled politician, who unleashes terrible passions and who brings war into a previously peaceful and undivided India'.[1]

What was the genesis of the movement for Pakistan? Could Gandhi have done anything to stave off the partition of India? What led to the terrible massacres and the mass migration of the minorities in 1947? Historians have been seeking answers to these questions; and though there can be no finality about the answers yet, we know enough to be able to form a reasonably clear picture of the course of events. For a just appraisal of these events, it is necessary to see them in the historical perspective.

The Hindu-Muslim problem, which culminated in the division of the subcontinent in 1947, long antedated Gandhi's advent on the Indian political scene. The Muslims, who constituted nearly one-fourth of the total population, differed from the Hindus in their religious tenets, usage, laws and customs; however, these differences were accepted and taken for granted by the two communities. During the Muslim rule, non-Muslims may have suffered at the hands of a whimsical or a fanatical ruler but, on the whole, the masses had learnt to live in a spirit of 'live and let live'. The evolution of a common language, dress and ceremonial in different parts of the country had assisted the process of adjustment. In fact, the cultural and social life of the two

communities differed not along communal but regional lines; a
Bengali Hindu was in many ways nearer a Bengali Muslim than
a Punjabi Hindu, and a Gujarati Muslim had more in common
with a Gujarati Hindu than with a Muslim from the South.

The British conquest of India placed the two communities on
a level—of common subjection—but as the process of conquest
had proceeded from the sea-coast inwards, it affected the Muslim
majority provinces of north-western India last of all. This
accident of history gave a start to the Hindus in acquiring
Western education and taking to modern commerce, and contributed to the emergence of a Hindu middle class subsisting on
government service, the professions and trade. The growth of
the Muslim middle class was slower. Muslim theologians, by
throwing their weight against Western education, further
handicapped Muslim youth in competing for government jobs.

In the closing decades of the nineteenth century the attitude
of the government to the Muslim community began to change.
The demand of the middle class, then necessarily Hindu in
composition, through the Indian National Congress for a larger
share in the government of the country brought about a new
orientation in the policy of the government. Muslims were
henceforth seen not as potential rebels but as probable allies.
To this reorientation, the Muslim leader who made the greatest
contribution was Syed Ahmad Khan. He tried to correct the
view of the Mutiny of 1857 as a Muslim revolt by recording the
services of Muslim nobles who had served the British government faithfully and well. He founded the Aligarh College and
the Muhammadan Educational Conference, and exhorted
Muslims to take advantage of Western education. There were
occasions when he criticized the government, but his criticisms
were discreet, and came from one whose loyalty was above
suspicion, and whose services were well rewarded by the government. Syed Ahmad Khan was nominated to the Imperial Legislative Council and the Public Service Commission, and granted
a knighthood.

Syed Ahmad Khan's main concern was the raising of his
community in the social and economic spheres. He did not want
Indian Muslims to be caught in the maelstrom of politics; this
was not only because he wished to cultivate British goodwill,
but also because he was afraid that a democratic system would

handicap Muslims. He exhorted them to keep away from the Indian National Congress. Thus he threw his powerful influence in favour of the isolation of his community from the nationalist movement just when this movement started on its career. He also raised the great question mark which was to shadow Indian politics for the next sixty years; what would be the position of the Muslim community in a free India? If British autocracy were to be replaced by an Indian democracy, would it give a permanent advantage to the Hindus, who heavily outnumbered the Muslims? Was it (as Syed Ahmad put it) a game of dice in which one man had four dice and the other only one? Had Muslims anything to gain from the withdrawal of British rule?

Nawab Viqar-ul-Mulk, another eminent Muslim educationist and politician, in opposing the setting up of elective institutions drew the stark moral for his co-religionists: 'We are numerically one-fifth of the other community. If at any time, the British Government ceases to exist in India we shall have to live as subjects of the Hindus . . . . If there is any device by which we can escape this, it is by the continuance of the British Raj, and our interests can be safeguarded only if we ensure the continuance of the British government'.[2]

There was only one possible answer which nationalists could give to the question as to how Muslims would fare in a free India: they would fare no better or no worse than the other communities. There was no reason to assume that in a free India political parties would follow communal affiliations, and that social or economic issues would not cut across religious divisions. A democratic system could embody the fullest guarantees of religious liberty, cultural autonomy and equal opportunity for all. Unfortunately, this line of thought could not be appreciated by those who were unable to visualize India of the future in any terms except those of the sordid present.

II

When, under the impact of the growing nationalist ferment in the country, the adoption of the elective principle became a live issue, a deputation of Muslim leaders, led by the Aga Khan, waited on the Viceroy, Lord Minto, in October 1906 and presented a memorial.

Most of the thirty-odd signatories to the memorial came from the titled and landed gentry, the Nawabs, the Khan Bahadurs and the C.I.E.s ('Companions of the Indian Empire'). The memorial included almost every demand that could possibly be made at that time upon the British government on behalf of the Muslim community *vis-à-vis* the Hindus. However, its primary object was to prevent the extension of the elective principle to the legislatures, and if that was not possible, to find some means of neutralizing the numerical inferiority of the Muslims. It was urged in the memorial that Muslim electors should form a separate electoral college of their own, and the Muslim community should be awarded more seats in expanded legislative councils than its numbers warranted. Minto, the Viceroy, in his reply appreciated 'the representative character of the deputation', and hailed his guests as 'the descendants of a conquering and ruling race'. He readily endorsed the thesis that representative institutions of the 'European type' were entirely new to the people of India, and their introduction required great care, forethought and caution. Above all, with unusual alacrity he conceded the major demands of the memorialists.

> The pith of your address, as I understand it, is a claim, that, in any system of representation, whether it affects a Municipality, a District Board, or a Legislature, in which it is proposed to introduce or increase an electoral organisation, the Mohammedan community should be represented as a community . . . . You justly claim that your position be estimated not merely on your numerical strength, but in respect to the political importance of your community and the service it has rendered to the Empire. I am entirely in accord with you.[3]

The leaders of the Muslim Deputation received encouragement and advice from Harcourt Butler, the Commissioner of Lucknow, who was soon to become a member of the Viceroy's Executive Council.[4] Principal Archbold of Aligarh College was already at Simla and had easy access to the private secretary to the Viceroy. It is difficult to guess Lord Minto's motives in giving wide-ranging assurances so hastily on constitutional issues, the full implications of which had yet to be worked out by the Government of India. The fact was that the Viceroy was under pressure from the nationalist elements in India and from the Liberal Secretary of State in London to initiate a scheme of constitutional reforms. He was not really convinced of the wisdom of such a scheme, but felt he could not stall it indefinitely. He and his advisers were thinking hard on how to offset any concession they might be compelled to make to nationalist opinion. Obviously it was in their interest to strengthen elements on whose loyalty they could count. The British policy-makers thus came to view the Muslim community in the same light as the princes and the landed class—as a possible 'counterpoise' to the Congress.

The Simla Deputation had more far-reaching consequences than its sponsors had dared to hope. Within three months of its meeting with the Viceroy the All-India Muslim League had been formed. Promotion of loyalty to the British government and protection and advancement of Muslim interests were the main objects of the new organization.

The political dividends of the Simla Deputation duly came in 1909 when separate electorates were incorporated in the Minto-Morley Reforms. The dangers of a separate register for a religious community were recognized by the authors of the Montagu-Chelmsford Reforms in their report nine years later:

> Division by creeds and classes means the creation of political camps organized against each other, and teaches men to think as partisans and not as citizens; it is difficult to see how the change from this system to national representation is ever to occur. The British Government is often accused of dividing men to govern them. But if it unnecessarily divided them at the very moment when it proposes to start them on the road to governing themselves, it will find it difficult to meet the charge of being hypocritical or short-sighted.

Nevertheless, separate electorates for the Muslim community came to stay; indeed they were extended to other communities, Sikhs, Christians, Europeans and Anglo-Indians. In 1916 they were embodied in the Lucknow Pact between the Indian National Congress and the Muslim League.

III

The Balkan Wars and the travail of Turkey in the years immediately preceding the First World War aroused anti-British feeling among Indian Muslims, and for a few years the Muslim

League came to be controlled by a Lucknow-based faction, with nationalist proclivities. This Hindu-Muslim rapprochement received a further boost after the war, when Gandhi lent his support to the Indian Muslims' demands for preserving the territorial integrity of Turkey and the preservation of the institution of the Caliphate.

In 1919–20, Hindu-Muslim unity reached its high watermark; the Khilafat movement became an integral part of Gandhi's campaign of non-co-operation with the government. It was not nationalist sentiment, but the concern for Turkey and the Holy Places of Islam, which provided the main impulse for this concordat between Muslims and Hindus. A common leadership could not make up for the essential divergence of ideals; while the Hindus thought in political terms of achieving self-government for India, the Khilafatists were preoccupied with the fate of Turkey. Muslim leaders denounced British imperialism, but based their denunciations on edicts issued by their *ulema*, the religious leaders. Deep and sincere as this religious emotion may have been, it was harnessed to a romantic cause, which was brought to an inglorious end by the Turks themselves when they abolished the institution of Sultan-Caliph. Gandhi's hope that the Hindus' spontaneous and altruistic gesture in supporting the cause of the Khilafat would permanently win the gratitude of the Muslim community was not to be realized. Thus the one successful experiment in bringing the Muslim community into the heart of the nationalist movement failed to break its psychological isolation, and indeed confirmed its tendency to view political problems from a religious angle.

When Gandhi came out of jail in 1924, he was shocked to see that the fabric of Hindu-Muslim unity, at which he had laboured so hard, had gone to pieces. There was an exceptional bitterness in communal controversies. His movement in 1919–23 had swept the lower middle class into the political vortex; communal politicians began to pander to this new audience. In this vulgarization of politics a section of the press, particularly the Indian language press took a notorious part. It was during this period that Gandhi described the newspaperman as 'a walking plague who spreads contagion of lies and calumnies'. He denounced communal madness; he appealed for human decency and tolerance; he fasted; he prayed. But it was all in vain. His voice,

once so powerful, was drowned in a din of communal recriminations by bigots on both sides.

A favourite solution in the nineteen-twenties was a communal pact through an 'All-Parties Conference'. There had
been a precedent in the Lucknow Pact of 1916. The argument
was that communal unity, once attained by the leaders, would
percolate to the masses. The sequence of these conferences
partook of the nature of a comic opera. Leaders of a number of
political parties and religious organizations would meet to the
accompaniment of sentimental effusions of goodwill. As they sat
down to allocate jobs under the government and seats in legislatures—the spoils of swaraj, as it were—they found it difficult
to reconcile their antagonistic claims. That such heterogeneous
groups should have been able to agree on anything was inconceivable, but there was a basic unreality about these discussions.
All the patronage and power which these leaders set out to
share was in fact controlled by the British government. Gandhi
disliked this pettifogging politics; he would have liked to disarm
Muslim fears by generosity on the part of the Hindus. Unfortunately, some Hindu politicians were as incapable of
generosity as the Muslim politicians were of trust. Moreover,
what was perhaps an insurance against future risk to the
Muslim, was seen as the thin end of the wedge by the Hindu.

The pattern of the unity conferences was nearly repeated at
the Round Table Conference in the early 1930s. Even the
second session in 1931, which was attended by Gandhi, failed to
bring off a solution acceptable to the motley group of delegates
whom the government had assembled in London. The squabbles
of the Round Table delegates were encouraged, if not wholly
manipulated, by the vested interests from India and the diehard
elements from Britain to prove to the world that it was Indian
disunity and not British reluctance which barred the path to
Indian self-government. Muslim leaders, such as the Aga Khan
and Sir Muhammad Shafi, were in close touch with Tory
politicians. Fazl-i-Husain, the Muslim member of the Viceroy's
Executive Council, pulled all the wires he could from Delhi to
prevent a compromise.[5]

Since constitution-making seemed to have foundered on the
lack of an agreement, the British government offered to impose
a solution. Ramsay MacDonald, the British Premier, issued a

Communal Award in 1933, laying down the quantum and mode of representation in legislatures. The perpetuation of separate electorates in the Communal Award was repugnant to the Indian National Congress; nevertheless, with Gandhi's approval, it was decided not to reject it until an alternative solution, acceptable to all the communities, could emerge.

IV

Even though the Communal Award had conceded almost all the political demands of the Muslim community, *vis-à-vis* the Hindus, Muslim politics continued to run in the old grooves. Far from being suppressed, the communal controversy raged like a hurricane during the next decade when Muslim separatism dominated and distorted the course of Indian politics. The central figure in Muslim politics during this crucial period was a brilliant lawyer and politician, M. A. Jinnah. He was six years younger than Gandhi, but was already a front-rank politician and parliamentarian when Gandhi came on the Indian scene. Like many other able and seasoned leaders of the Moderate Era, Jinnah found himself in the shade when Gandhi stole the limelight. In the mid-twenties, Jinnah led an independent group in the Central Legislative Assembly, where he held the balance between the government and the Swaraj Party of the Congress: this was a role which he could play with masterly skill. His opposition to the solution of the communal problem proposed in the Nehru Report went a long way to kill it in 1928. To Gandhi's civil disobedience movement in 1930 he took no more kindly than he had done ten years earlier to the non-co-operation movement. At the Round Table Conference he ploughed a lonely furrow, and when it was over, he was so disgusted that he bade good-bye to politics and settled down in London to practise at the English Bar. But when the time came for the general elections under the new constitution, he returned to India and led the Muslim League to the polls. The results of the elections in 1937 came as a great blow to him. His party secured less than 5 per cent of the Muslim votes. It won thirty-nine out of 117 Muslim seats in Bengal (where there was no chance of a Congress ministry), but only one seat in the Punjab out of eighty-four Muslim seats, and three in Sind out of thirty-three Muslim

seats. It did not win a single Muslim seat in the provincial
legislatures of Bihar, Central Provinces and Orissa. In Madras,
it won ten seats, in Bombay twenty. In the U.P. it won twenty-
seven of the sixty-four Muslim seats in a House of 228 members,
while the Congress won 133 seats.

It is obvious that with this poor showing, the League hardly
qualified for a coalition in most of the provinces. Only in one
province, that is, the United Provinces, there were serious
negotiations for a coalition. It has been suggested that the
Congress committed a great blunder by refusing a coalition,
which fanned the fires of Muslim frustration, which in turn
fuelled the movement for Pakistan. Maulana Azad's assertion
in his autobiography that if the Congress had been generous
enough to offer two seats (instead of one) to the Muslim League
in the U.P. cabinet, the Muslim League party in the provinces
would have disintegrated, and the demand for Pakistan would
not have arisen 'is too naive to merit consideration'.[6] It is
certainly true that a few Muslim Leaguers in U.P., such as
Khaliquzzaman and Nawab Ismail Khan, who were eager for a
partnership with the Congress, and felt affronted in these negotiations, later became Jinnah's right-hand men in his anti-
Congress campaign. But the question of a coalition in 1937 was
not as simple a matter as it has been made out. Some of the
Congress leaders in U.P. feared that if the Muslim League, with
its feudal and landlord support, was brought into the ministry,
the Congress agrarian programme, particularly the abolition of
landlordism, would be in jeopardy. That this fear was not
groundless was proved by the stubborn opposition of the Muslim
League party to land reforms in the U.P. legislature during the
years 1937–46.

No one could say in the summer of 1937 how the Congress
would hit it off with the British bureaucracy, which until recently
had been its arch enemy. The Congress approach to office
acceptance in 1937 was marked by a measure of caution and
reserve. A very important consideration for the Congress was
whether the provincial cabinet, after the induction of the League
members, would be able to maintain its cohesion. The Congress
and the League represented two contradictory urges. The
Congress stood for democracy, socialism and a common Indian
nationality; the League existed to promote the interests of

Muslims in India as a separate political entity. Jinnah spoke of his desire for a settlement with the Congress, but on his own terms: a weak centre, complete autonomy for the provinces, shares of the Muslims in the services, elected bodies and cabinets to be fixed by statute, and recognition of the Muslim League as the sole representative of the Muslim community. He wanted the Congress to keep its hands off the Muslims and admit itself as a Hindu body. Even if the U.P. League leaders had been able to reach an agreement with the Congress, they would have been repudiated by Jinnah, who was the president of the All-India Muslim League, and was determined to keep the reins of the League firmly in his hands. Jinnah had indeed threatened Khaliquzzaman, the main League negotiator in the United Provinces, with disciplinary action if he persisted in an isolated and piecemeal agreement with the Congress.

It is impossible to understand the history of the communal problem during the next ten years without taking into account Jinnah's personality and methods. As Professor Khalid B. Sayeed says, Jinnah was a 'superb tactician' and the various moves that he made were all parts of a 'master plan, the supreme objective of which was the accumulation and concentration of enormous power in his hands, an objective, which he could rationalize in terms of the well-being and social goals of the Muslim nation and Pakistan'.[7]

Jinnah had met with an electoral disaster of the first magnitude in 1937. Not only had the Muslim electorate failed to vote his party to office in the Muslim-majority provinces, but even in the Muslim-minority provinces, his party had been routed. It seemed he could do little to improve his position until the next round of elections. Jinnah was, however, not the man to let history pass over his head. He set out to achieve through a propaganda blast what the ballot box had denied him.

Jinnah, who was 61 in 1937, had his roots in the Victorian age and had been trained as a nationalist and constitutionalist in the school of Dadabhai Naoroji and Gokhale. But he decided to use the dynamite of religious emotion to acquire political influence and power. Jawaharlal Nehru was horrified when during a bye-election in U.P. in 1937, Jinnah appealed in the name of Allah and the Holy Koran for support of the Muslim League candidate. 'To exploit the name of God and religion in an

election context', Nehru declared, 'is an extraordinary thing . . .
even for a humble canvasser. For Mr. Jinnah to do so is inexpli-
cable. I would beg him to consider this aspect of the question . . . .
It means rousing religious and communal passions in political
matters; it means working for the Dark Age in India'.[8]

Nehru's appeal was in vain. The Congress ministries had not
been in office even for a few weeks, when Jinnah was proclaiming
that Muslims could not expect any justice or fair-play at their
hands. Nearly half the members of the I.C.S. were still British;
they occupied the key positions in the provincial secretariat,
besides holding charge of important districts. Almost all the
Inspectors-General of Police were British, and so were most of
the district superintendents of police. There was a fair sprinkling
of Muslims and Christians in the I.C.S., and Muslims were
rather well represented in the middle and lower ranks of the
police. Law and order was a provincial subject, but the channels
of communication between the Viceroy and his colleagues in
the executive council of the one hand, and the British Governors
and chief secretaries in the provinces on the other, had not dried
up. And yet there is no evidence in the records of the Government
of India of a concerted tyranny against Muslims in the Congress-
governed provinces. The Congress suggested an inquiry by Sir
Maurice Gwyer, the Chief Justice of the Federal Court, but the
proposal was turned down by the Muslim League. The fact is
that the bogey of a Congress tyranny was raised not to convince
the British government or the Hindus, but to work upon the
feelings of the Muslim masses.

What was this Congress tyranny against which Jinnah was
protesting? One of the grievances was that excessive reverence
was paid to Gandhi, and that his birthday had been declared a
holiday. 'To declare my birthday as a holiday', commented
Gandhi, 'should be classified as a cognisable offence'. Another
grievance was the use of the Congress flag on government
buildings. The Congress flag was born during the days of the
Khilafat movement, and its colours had been determined to
represent the various communities: saffron for the Hindus,
green for Muslims and white for other minorities. Objections
were raised by the League to the *Bande Mataram* song on the
ground that its original context in a novel by the nineteenth-
century Bengali novelist, Bankim Chandra Chatterji, had

communal overtones. The song had first become popular during
the agitation against the partition of Bengal, when it came to be
regarded by the British as a symbol of sedition. From 1905 to
1920, the song had been sung at innumerable Congress meetings
at which Jinnah himself had been present. Nevertheless, out of
deference to Muslim susceptibilities, the Congress Working
Committee decided that only the first two stanzas should be
sung on ceremonial occasions. Gandhi's advice to Congressmen
was not to sing the *Bande Mataram* or hoist the Congress flag if a
single Muslim objected.

One of the targets of the League criticism was the Wardha
Scheme of Basic Education which had been devised largely by
two eminent Muslim educationists, Zakir Husain and K. G.
Saiyidain, to substitute a coordinated training in the use of the
hand and the eye for a notoriously bookish and volatile learning
which village children unlearned after leaving school. The
complaint that the scheme did not provide for religious instruction of Muslim children had little meaning, because the curri-
culum did not include such instruction for any community.

When Nehru returned after a brief visit to Europe in 1938, he
was struck by the similarity between the propaganda methods
of the Muslim League in India and of the Nazis in Germany:
'The League leaders had begun to echo the Fascist tirade
against democracy . . . Nazis were wedded to a negative policy.
So also was the League. The League was anti-Hindu, anti-
Congress, anti-national . . . . The Nazis raised the cry of hatred
against the Jews, the League [had] raised [its] cry against the
Hindus.'

V

The cry of Islam in danger, the reiteration of 'Congress tyranny',
and the spectre of 'Hindu Raj' widened the communal gulf and
created the climate in which the proposal for the partition of the
country could be mooted. Jinnah propounded his two-nation
theory. He argued that the differences between Hindus and
Muslims were not only confined to religion, but covered the
whole range of their social, cultural and economic life. He
asserted that India was not one nation, that the Muslims of
India constituted a separate nation, and were, therefore, entitled

to a separate homeland of their own where they could work out their destiny. In March 1940, this theory was embodied in the famous Pakistan resolution of the All-India Muslim League, which declared that no constitutional plan for India would be workable or acceptable to Muslims unless it was based on a demarcation of Muslim majority areas in the north-west and the east as independent states.

The rationale of the two-nation theory was dubious. If religion was the criterion of nationality, and each nationality was to be allowed a homeland for itself, would it not mean the 'balkaniza-tion' of India? If non-Muslims were to continue staying in the future Pakistan—as the League leaders assured they would—how would the new state be different? If Hindus and Muslims were two separate nations, which could not live peacefully in India, how would they become a peaceful nation in Pakistan? If democracy did not suit India, how would it become suitable for Pakistan? Would not partition of the country further weaken the position of the minority *vis-à-vis* the majority in each of the successor states?

Gandhi's first reaction to the two-nation theory and the demand for Pakistan was one of bewilderment, almost of incredulity. Was it the function of religion to separate men or to unite them? He described the two-nation theory as an untruth; in his dictionary there was no stronger word. He discussed the attributes of nationality. The vast majority of Muslims of India were converts to Islam, or were the descendants of converts. A change of religion did not change nationality; the religious divisions did not coincide with cultural differences. A Bengali Muslim, he wrote, 'speaks the same tongue that a Bengali Hindu does, eats the same food, has the same amusements as his Hindu neighbour. They dress alike . . . . His [Jinnah's] name could be that of any Hindu. When I first met him, I did not know he was a Muslim'.

To divide India was to undo the centuries of work done by Hindus and Muslims; Gandhi's soul rebelled against the idea that Hinduism and Islam represented antagonistic cultures and doctrines, and that eighty million Muslims had really nothing in common with their Hindu neighbours. And even if there were religious and cultural differences, what clash of interests could there be on such matters as revenue, industry, sanitation or justice? The differences could only be in religious doctrine and observances with which a secular state should have no concern.

Until almost the last stage, Jinnah did not define the boundaries nor fill in the outlines of his Pakistan proposal; each of his followers was thus free to see Pakistan in his own image. The orthodox dreamt of a state reproducing the purity of pristine Islam. Those with a secular outlook hoped for tangible benefits from their 'own' state. The Pakistan idea sold fast with the Muslim community. The Muslim middle class, which for historical reasons had been left behind in the race for the plums of government service, trade and industry in certain areas, was attracted by the idea of a sovereign Muslim state. Muslim landlords in Bengal and Punjab saw the prospect of deliverance from 'progressive politicians' like Jawaharlal Nehru who indulged in the dangerous talk of abolishing zamindari. Muslim officials were glad of the new vistas which were expected to open to them in a new state, without the Hindu seniors hovering over their heads. Muslim traders and industrialists began to cherish visions of free fields for their prosperous ventures without the intrusion of Hindu competitors.

Ever since the days of Syed Ahmad Khan the Muslim community had been exhorted by its prominent leaders to keep away from anti-British movements. Those who gave and those who followed this advice had a guilty feeling in the deeper recesses of their hearts. The Pakistan idea for the first time seemed to satisfy the religious emotions as well as the political instincts of the Muslim middle class. The vision of a sovereign Muslim state in India was reminiscent of the past glories of Muslim rule; it was too fascinating a prospect not to catch the popular imagination.[9] The Muslim intellectual felt a new exhilaration for a programme which promised independence from both the British and the Hindus; the fact that it brought his community into collision with the majority community and not with the British only made the movement somewhat less hazardous.

The outbreak of the World War in 1939 helped the propagation of the separatist ideology. The resignation of the Congress ministries in eight out of eleven provinces came as a god-send to the Muslim League. If the Congress ministries had remained in office, the atrocity stories against them could not have been repeated without being challenged. As it was, the Viceroy and the British Governors of the various provinces could hardly be expected to give a 'clearance certificate' to those who had now become their political opponents. The war itself was an important consideration for not alienating the Muslim League. The Viceroy and his advisers, anticipating a show-down with the Congress, were in search of friends. The demand for Pakistan probably surprised them as much as it had surprised the Congress. Initially, its significance in British eyes was that it confirmed their stock thesis that the constitutional progress of India was impeded not by British hesitation but by Indian disunity. Linlithgow's declaration in August 1940 that 'it goes without saying that . . . [the British government] could not contemplate transfer of their present responsibilities for the peace and welfare of India to any system of government whose authority is directly denied by large and powerful elements in India's national life' was the first tacit recognition that the British were prepared to consider even such drastic solutions as Jinnah had propounded. The Pakistan resolution of the All-India Muslim League had only been passed in March 1940; but for the war, it is doubtful if even an indirect official acknowledgement of the Pakistan proposal would have been made within five months.

VI

In a perceptive analysis of Jinnah's 'chess-board-like strategy',[10] Khalid B. Sayeed shows how the League leader strengthened his own position and that of his party by the 'tactical moves' he made, and by exploiting the 'wrong moves' made by his opponents.[11] He kept Congress leaders on tenterhooks by pretending to negotiate with them when he had no intention of doing so. He was careful not to embroil himself with the British, but he did not offer his full co-operation to them either. He outwitted and outmanoeuvred such seasoned Muslim politicians as Sikander Hyat Khan and Fazl-ul-Haq. When the Congress went into the political wilderness with the Quit India movement in 1942 and most of the Congress members of provincial legislatures were in jail, Jinnah, with the help of the British Governors, succeeded in installing Muslim League ministries in Assam, North-West Frontier Province, Sind and Bengal. From every attempt at a solution of the constitutional deadlock between 1939 and 1946, he was able to extract political gains for himself and his party. The Cripps Mission in 1942 mattered to him only in so far as the provision for the non-accession of provinces signified an indirect endorsement of the 'principle' of partition. The ill-fated Bhulabhai-Liaqat Ali Pact was repudiated by him, but it introduced the idea of parity between the Congress and the League in the Interim Government. The Gandhi-Jinnah talks in 1944 were useful to the League leader only in so far as they raised his prestige with his own following. It was his veto which made the Simla Conference in 1945 a futile exercise. In 1946 he played a crucial role in the negotiations conducted by the Cabinet Mission; in 1947 his consent was essential for the June 3 plan which decided in favour of the division of the country.

There is no doubt that Jinnah played his game of political chess with great skill. By arousing deep emotions, by avoiding the elucidation of his demand for Pakistan, and by concentrating on a tirade against 'Hindu Raj' and 'Congress tyranny', he was able to create and sustain a large consensus in his own community. By keeping his cards close to his chest, he was able to keep his following in good order. Such was the magical effect of his insistence on 'the full, six provinces Pakistan' that large numbers of his adherents in Bengal and the Punjab failed to see that the division of India would also mean the division of these two provinces. Even Suhrawardy, an astute politician, who headed the League Ministry in Bengal, confessed later that he had not expected the partition of Bengal.[12] As for Muslims in the Hindu-majority provinces, they had in any case little to gain from the secession of the Muslim-majority provinces in the east and west; the two-nation theory and the theory of hostages could do them no good at all.

From near political elipse in 1935 Jinnah had, within a decade, brought his party to a position where it could decisively influence events. The final result, the partition of India, was doubtless a personal triumph for him. His success was, however, due not only to his own skill and tenacity, but to the tension between the Congress and the government. It is not surprising that in their long-drawn-out struggle with the Indian National Congress, the British came to have a soft corner for the Muslim League. They were glad to use Muslim separatism—just as they used the princely order—to spike the nationalist guns. As Peter Hardy points out in his scholarly study of Muslim politics in India, 'to expect them [the British] to encourage the ideals and the growth of non-communal nationalism and thus to hasten their own demise as the rulers of India, with all that would mean for the British political and economic position in the world, was to expect a degree not merely of altruism, but also of prophetic insight out of the world of the history of governments'.[13]

The antagonism between the Congress and the British government helped the Muslim League in two ways, in securing it at crucial moments the support of certain British politicians and civil servants, and in ensuring to the League the exclusive possession of the Indian political stage when the Congress was outlawed. The brunt of the struggle for liberation of India was borne by the Congress. The Muslim League had no lot or part in this struggle, of which the establishment of Pakistan was a by-product. Others forced open the door through which Jinnah walked to his goal.

VII

How far were the Indian National Congress and Gandhi responsible for the partition of the country? As we have seen, Muslim separatism came into existence almost simultaneously with the birth of the Congress. The question of safeguards for minorities, and especially for the Muslim community, dominated Indian politics for decades. Gandhi and his adherents in the Congress believed that religion is not a satisfactory basis for nationality in the modern world, that multi-religious, multi-lingual and multi-racial societies should seek political solutions for co-existence within the framework of a federal structure. This was what had been done under widely different conditions by the U.S.A., U.S.S.R. and Canada. But the Congress position was far from inflexible on this issue; indeed from the acceptance of separate electorates in the Lucknow Pact in 1916 to the acquiescence in the Communal Award in 1933, and finally to the Cabinet Mission Plan in 1946, it was a continual retreat in the face of Muslim pressure. Some of the Hindu leaders tended to be niggardly, yielding to Muslim demands step by step, but there was no fixity in Muslim claims either. Jinnah's price for a communal settlement rose progressively. Beginning with separate electorates in 1916, it went up to Fourteen Points in 1929, to composite ministries in 1937, and finally to the partition of the country in 1940. The six provinces he claimed for Pakistan included Assam, where the Muslim population was 33 per cent, and the whole of the Punjab and Bengal, where the Muslim majority was slight indeed. And when the partition of the country had been agreed to, he claimed a land corridor to connect the eastern and western arms of Pakistan.[14]

As we have seen, Gandhi opposed the two-nation theory and the division of India, but he had written as early as April 1940: 'I know no non-violent method of compelling the obedience of eight crores of Muslims to the will of the rest of India, however powerful a majority the rest may represent. The Muslims must have the same right of self-determination that the rest of India has. We are at present a joint family. Any member may claim a division'.[15] This was a perfectly logical position for a leader, who was committed to non-violence to adopt, but another leader, following the example of Abraham Lincoln, may have insisted that there could be no compromise on the unity of the country.

In 1942, the Congress Working Committee, in its resolution on the Cripps Mission affirmed that 'it could not think in terms of compelling the people of any territorial unit to remain in the Indian Union against their declared and established will'. Two years later, in his talks with Jinnah, Gandhi not only accepted the principle of Pakistan, but even discussed the mechanism for the demarcation of the boundaries between the two successor states. In 1946, after much heart-searching, the Congress accepted the Cabinet Mission Plan with a three-tier structure and a central government limited to control over defence, foreign affairs and communications. It was a delicate constitutional framework with numerous checks and balances; unless the two major parties entered the Constituent Assembly with goodwill it was impossible to draft a workable constitution, much less to work it. Of this goodwill there was no sign.

It has been suggested that the last chance of maintaining the unity of India was lost in July 1946 when Jawaharlal Nehru addressed the All-India Congress Committee and a press conference at Bombay. His 'intemperate remarks' are alleged to have led to the withdrawal of the Muslim League from the Cabinet Mission Plan.[16]

A careful study of Jawaharlal Nehru's speech at the meeting of the Congress Party shows that Nehru was replying to the criticism levelled by left-wing critics in the party who had questioned the status and power of the Constituent Assembly, on the ground that it was being convened by the British government and could exist only on its sufferance. The oft-quoted sentence from this speech, 'We are not bound by a single thing except that we have decided to go to the Constituent Assembly', was not the most important part of it; it was intended to parry the critics within the Congress Party and not to provoke the Muslim League. The whole tenor of Nehru's long speech was a justification of the Congress acceptance of the Cabinet Mission Plan. He refuted the charge that the Constituent Assembly would be a sham, or a nursery game at which Indian politicians would play while the British government supervised them. And at his press conference three days later, while Nehru emphasized the sovereign character of the Constituent Assembly, he also affirmed that the Congress was determined to make a success of the constitutional mechanism outlined by the Cabinet Mission. While Nehru had emphasized that the formation of groups in the Cabinet Mission Plan was not compulsory, he had not repudiated the procedure laid down in the Plan.[17]

The Muslim League professed to be offended by Nehru's remarks, and passed a resolution withdrawing its acceptance of the Cabinet Mission Plan. As Pethick-Lawrence, the Secretary of State for India, told an Indian visitor, 'these remarks gave Jinnah the excuse he was looking for to get out of the Constituent Assembly and the Cabinet Mission Plan'.[18] The fact is that the League had never really accepted the Plan; its resolution affirmed that 'the Muslim League agreed to cooperate with the constitution-making machinery proposed in the scheme outlined by the Mission in the hope that it would ultimately result in the establishment of a complete sovereign Pakistan'. Clearly, the League did not treat the Cabinet Mission Plan, with its three-tier structure, as a final compromise between the Congress ideal of a strong, united India, and the League objective of two separate sovereign states. Jinnah and other League leaders made no secret of their design to make the groups of provinces (which included large contiguous Hindu-majority areas in West Bengal, in East Punjab and Assam) as a prelude to secession and formation of an independent state. The Congress leaders had, of course, no intention of letting the Muslim League get away with the 'full six province Pakistan' of its conception by disguising them in the first instance as 'groups of provinces'. It is doubtful if the Cabinet Mission Plan could have preserved the unity of India; it would have only given to the Muslim League 'a "big" Pakistan through the back door, and left India with a weak minimal centre'.[19]

Recent research has tended to confirm the view that Jinnah's demand for Pakistan was no bargaining counter,[20] that he was bent upon the creation of sovereign states in the west and the east, and that he would have treated any compromise with the Congress only as a stepping-stone to further demands. The limit of constitutional concessions had long since been reached; any further concessions would have handicapped the future Indian state, without preventing the secession of the Muslim-majority regions.

The Interim Government in 1946–7 at the centre revealed the utter incompatibility of the Congress and the Muslim League. The communal riots, which began at Calcutta on 16 August 1946, spread like a prairie fire from Calcutta to East Bengal, from East Bengal to Bihar, and from Bihar to the Punjab. India seemed to be sliding into an undeclared civil war with battle lines passing through almost every town and village. Split from top to bottom, the Interim Government was unable to set an example of cohesion or firmness. The Viceroy seemed to have been outplayed in the face of divergent pressures which he could neither reconcile nor control; he suggested to his superiors in London the desperate expedient of a British evacuation of India, province by province. To check the drift to chaos, Prime Minister Attlee came to the conclusion that what was needed was a new policy and a new Viceroy to carry it out. June 1948 was announced as the latest date for termination of British rule in India, and Mountbatten was appointed to succeed

Wavell in March 1947. Mountbatten's task was facilitated by the fact that by March 1947, most Congress leaders, including Nehru and Patel, had reconciled themselves to the partition of India. They had been chastened by their experience of working with the Muslim League in the Interim Government as well as by the growing lawlessness in the country. The choice seemed to them to be between anarchy and partition; they resigned themselves to the latter in order to salvage three-fourths of India from the chaos which threatened the whole. The decision in favour of the partition was not that of only Nehru and Patel; in the All-India Congress Committee 157 voted for and only fifteen against it.

Gandhi took little part in the final negotiations, but his opposition to partition was an open secret. 'We are unable to think coherently', he declared, 'whilst the British power is still functioning in India. Its function is not to change the map of India. All it has to do is to withdraw and leave India, carrying out the withdrawal, if possible, in an orderly manner, may be even in chaos, on or before the promised date'. The very violence, which in the opinion of his Congress colleagues and that of the British government provided a compelling motive for partition, was for him an irresistible argument against it; to accept partition because of the fear of civil war was to acknowledge that 'everything was to be got if mad violence was perpetrated in sufficient measure'.

Gandhi was convinced that the communal tension however serious it seemed in 1947 was a temporary phase, and that the British had no right to impose partition 'on an India temporarily gone mad'. His plea that there should be 'peace before Pakistan' was not acceptable to the Muslim League. In fact the League's case was that there could be no peace until Pakistan was established. Having declared their resolve to quit India by June 1948, the British did not want to—and perhaps could not—antagonize the Muslim League. Three or four years earlier they could have exercised a moderating influence on the League; in 1947, the scope for this influence was strictly limited. The sins of Linlithgow and Churchill were visited on Mountbatten and Attlee.

CHAPTER 12

The Partition Massacres

The Muslim League had insisted that there could be no peace in India until its demand for the creation of a separate Muslim state was conceded. The Mountbatten Plan of June 1947, which provided for two new Dominions to come into existence from 15 August 1947, conceded this demand. After its acceptance by the British government, the Indian National Congress and the All-India Muslim League, the plan was expected to usher in an era of communal amity in the subcontinent. To the consternation of the British government and the Indian political leaders, what actually ensued was violence on an unprecedented scale, compelling the minorities—the Hindus in West Pakistan and the Muslims in East Punjab—to flee for safety across the newly created border between the two states.

The communal violence, which flared up in August–September 1947, was part of the chain-reaction which had begun a year earlier with the terrible riot in Calcutta on 16 August 1946, which had been observed by the Muslim League as the Direct Action Day. The provocation for this observance had been the decision of the Viceroy, Lord Wavell, to form an Interim Government with the representatives of the Congress, even though the Muslim League was not prepared to join it. Nehru went to see Jinnah, but the League leader declined to co-operate. Jinnah thundered against 'the caste Hindu, Fascist Congress . . . who want to be installed in power and authority of the Government of India to dominate and rule over the Mussalmans . . . with the aid of British bayonets'.[1] He held out the threat of 'direct action'. 'This day', said Jinnah, 'we bid good-bye to constitutional methods . . . . Today we have also forged a pistol and are in a position to use it'.[2] The Congress had resorted to 'direct action' on a number of occasions against the government in the past, but in each case it had been under Gandhi's direction, and Gandhi's adherence to non-violence was clear beyond any doubt. No other Congress leader had ever ventured to launch a mass movement. Evidently, Jinnah and his colleagues in the Muslim League did not realize the implications of a campaign of 'direct action'; it needed something more than angry words and menacing gestures.

On the 'Direct Action Day', 16 August 1946, Calcutta witnessed a communal riot to which the *Statesman* gave the grim epithet of 'The Great Calcutta Killing'. For four days, bands of hooligans armed with sticks, spears, hatchets and even firearms roamed the town, robbing and killing at will. More than five thousand lives were lost and the number of injured was estimated at fifteen thousand. Bengal was at this time ruled by a Muslim League ministry headed by H. S. Suhrawardy. It was alleged that he had deliberately prevented the police from acting promptly and impartially. If—as was suggested at the time—the outbreak was intended to serve as a demonstration of the strength of the Muslim feeling on the demand for Pakistan, it turned out to be a double-edged weapon. The non-Muslims of Calcutta reeled under the initial blow, but then, taking advantage of their numerical superiority, hit back savagely. The impression went abroad that, in spite of a Muslim League ministry in Bengal, the Hindus had won in the trial of strength at Calcutta. Two months later reprisals followed in the Muslim-majority districts of Noakhali in East Bengal where, exploiting poor communications, and encouraged by fanatical mullahs and ambitious politicians, local hooligans burnt the Hindus' property, looted their crops, desecrated their temples, kidnapped Hindu women and made forcible conversions. Thousands of Hindus fled from their homes.

Gandhi was in Delhi when the news from East Bengal came through. He was particularly hurt by the crimes against women. He cancelled all his plans and decided to leave for East Bengal. Friends tried to dissuade him. His health was poor; important political developments, on which his advice would be required, were imminent. 'I do not know', he said, 'what I shall be able to do there [in East Bengal]. All that I know is that I won't be at peace unless I go'.

At Calcutta he saw the ravages of the August riot and confessed to 'a sinking feeling at the mass madness which can turn a man into a brute'. He made a courtesy call on the British Governor, and talked to Premier Suhrawardy and his colleagues and to Hindu and Muslim leaders. He made it clear that he was interested not in finding out which community was to blame, but in creating conditions which would enable the two communities to resume their peaceful life. To Professor N. K. Bose, who acted as his secretary during his stay in East Bengal, Gandhi confided his strategy: 'The first thing is that politics have divided India today into Hindus and Muslims. I want to rescue people from this quagmire and make them work on solid ground where people are people. Therefore my appeal here is not to the Muslims as Muslims, nor to Hindus as Hindus, but to ordinary human beings who have to keep their villages clean, to build schools for their children and take many other steps so that they can make life better.'[3]

II

The atmosphere in East Bengal was charged with suspicion, fear, hatred and violence. Gandhi took his residence in Srirampur, one of the worst hit villages. He saw gaping walls, gutted roofs, charred ruins and remnants of skeletons in the debris, the handiwork of religious frenzy. He embarked on a village-to-village tour. He discarded his sandals and, like the pilgrims of old, walked barefoot. The village tracks were slippery and sometimes maliciously strewn with brambles and broken glass; the fragile bamboo bridges were tricky to negotiate.

His presence acted as a soothing balm on the countryside; it eased tension, assuaged anger and softened tempers. His success would have been more spectacular were it not for the propaganda against him in the Muslim press, alleging a 'deep political game' behind his mission. Under pressure from local party bosses—and perhaps from the League High Command—Premier Suhrawardy became critical of Gandhi's tour and joined in the outcry that he should quit Bengal. Gandhi was not dismayed by this perverse opposition; he argued that, if he could not command the confidence of the Muslim League leaders, the responsibility was his own. An entry in his diary, dated 2 January 1947, reads: 'Have been awake since 2 a.m.

God's grace alone is sustaining me . . . . All round me is utter darkness. When will God take me out of this darkness into His light?"[4]

Meanwhile the Hindu peasantry of Bihar wreaked a terrible vengeance on the Muslim minority in that province for the events in East Bengal. Early in March Gandhi moved over to Bihar where his refrain was the same as in East Bengal: the majority must repent and make amends; the minority must forget and forgive and make a fresh start. He would not accept any apology for communal madness, and chided those who sought in the misdeeds of the rioters in East Bengal a justification for reprisals in Bihar. Civilized conduct, he insisted, was the duty of every individual irrespective of what others did.

In March 1947 news of serious disturbances came from the Punjab. The Muslim League's 'direct action' campaign to dislodge the Unionist-Akali-Congress coalition sparked off a conflagration in that province; the Hindu and Sikh minorities in its western districts went through the same horrors as the Muslim minority in Bihar and the Hindu minority in East Bengal. A semblance of order was restored with the help of the army, but tension continued. The first two towns of the Punjab, Lahore and Amritsar, were caught up in a strange guerilla warfare in which shooting, stabbing and arson went on in the midst of police patrols and curfew orders.

III

Gandhi was in Bihar when he received the news of the trouble in the Punjab. Since October 1946 he had been wandering from one province to another in a vain attempt to stem the tide of violence. For Gandhi this violence was a shocking, and even a bewildering phenomenon. All his life he had worked for the day when India would set an example of non-violence to the world. The chasm between what he had cherished in his heart and what he saw was so great that he could not help feeling a deep sense of failure. His first impulse was to blame himself. Had he been unobservant, careless, indifferent, impatient? Had he failed to detect in time that while the people on the whole refrained from overt violence in the struggle against foreign rule, they continued to harbour ill-feeling against the British? Was communal violence only an expression of the violence which had smouldered in the breasts of those who had paid lip-service to non-violence?

In retrospect it would appear that Gandhi was exaggerating his own responsibility and the failure of non-violence. It was remarkable enough that in the several satyagraha campaigns he had led, violence had been reduced to negligible proportions, and India's millions received a political awakening without that heavy dose of hatred against Britain and the British people that is commonly associated with resurgent nationalism.

The real explanation for the violence of 1946–7 is to be sought in the tensions which the Muslim League's seven-year-long campaign for Pakistan aroused in its protagonists as well as opponents. The basic premise of this campaign was that Hindus and Muslims had nothing in common in the past or the present. Millions of people were seized with vague hopes and fears. No one could say with certainty whether India would survive as one country, or would be divided into two or more states, whether the Punjab or Bengal would be split, whether the princely states would be integrated into an independent India, or become autonomous units. The *adivasis* of Central India and the Nagas of Assam suddenly found champions for an independence which they had never claimed before; there was talk of a Dravidistan in the South, and a thousand-mile corridor to link the two wings of the future Pakistan. We now know that the Nizam of Hyderabad with the backing of some Conservative politicians in London was intriguing with the Portuguese to secure an access to the sea-port of Goa,[5] so as to be able to set himself up as an independent sultan after the British withdrawal. The rulers of several other states such as Travancore and Bhopal entertained similar, grandiose ambitions. All this could not but excite popular fantasy; the turbulent elements began to see in the coming transfer of power a period of power vacuum such as had occurred in the twilight of the Mughal empire.

In the face of these perils the Government of India was an uneasy coalition of the Congress and the Muslim League—and the provincial governments faced increasing demoralization. British officers, with the imminent termination of their careers, had neither the ability nor perhaps the will to cope with the volcanic violence which was erupting. Indian officers, when they were themselves free from the communal virus, found it difficult to restrain their subordinates. The growth of private armies, the Muslim League National Guards, the Rashtriya Swayam Sevak Sangh and others, showed that popular faith in the impartiality of the instruments of law and order was at a discount.

Since October 1946 Gandhi had made the assuaging of communal fanaticism his primary mission. His tours of Bengal and Bihar succeeded in re-educating the masses to some extent, but he was handicapped by the fact that his voice did not carry the weight with the Muslim intelligentsia which it had once done. If his efforts at restoring communal peace had been supplemented by someone who commanded the allegiance of the Muslim community, his task would not have been half so difficult. If Jinnah had toured East Bengal or West Punjab, he might have helped in stopping the rot. Such a suggestion would, however, have been simply laughed away by the League leader; consummate politician as he was, his political instincts rebelled against fasts and walking tours. After the 'Great Calcutta Killing' and the disturbances in Bengal, Bihar and the Punjab, communal violence became the strongest argument in the Muslim League's brief for Pakistan. Its leaders insisted that the choice lay between 'a divided or a destroyed India'.

IV

The Mountbatten Plan had fixed 15 August as the date for the simultaneous transfer of power from Britain to India and the partition of the country. Two and a half months were obviously too short a period for such a vast and complex undertaking. The Viceroy and his advisers worked overtime to deal with the numerous constitutional and administrative issues. The Congress and the League leaders were confronted with the prodigious task of dividing the assets of a state apparatus which had been built up for a century and a half as a unitary government. The integration of 562 Indian states in the new political framework was itself a formidable problem. But the most critical decision, of which the full implications do not seem to have been realized at the time, was to divide the civil services and the armed forces between the two successor-states.

Early in April 1947 General Auchinleck, the British Commander-in-Chief, wrote that it would take five to ten years to divide the Indian army.[6] Mountbatten warned Jinnah that the sudden withdrawal of British officers from the Indian army was a serious enough step, but to further synchronize it with the splitting of the army on a religious basis was to subject it to an impossible strain. This dual reorganization was fraught with great risks, as the army was likely to be out of action for at least some time. Jinnah did not heed Mountbatten's warning and insisted on the division of the armed forces and the administrative services.

The final decision to split the army was taken on 30 June, just six weeks before the transfer of power.[7] The division was to be on the basis of domicile, although Muslim personnel of Indian domicile could opt for the Pakistan army and Hindu personnel of Pakistan domicile could opt for the Indian army. As the Muslim component of the armed forces, other than the navy, was drawn largely from West Pakistan districts, in effect the division of the forces was on communal lines. Pending the complete reshuffling of the armed forces, it was decided to effect a rough and ready division, that is, to ensure immediate movement of all Muslim-majority military units to Pakistan and of all non-Muslim majority units to India.

Simultaneously, steps were taken to divide the administrative services on a religious basis. The civilian officials of the central government were given the option to select the government they wished to serve. This option was later extended to the employees of the provincial governments of the Punjab, Bengal and Assam. An overwhelming majority of Hindu and Sikh officials opted for India at the central level and for West Bengal, East Punjab and Assam at the provincial level; the vast majority of Muslim officials opted for Pakistan. In July 1947 orders were issued to arrange, as far as possible, transfers in accordance with the options of the employees before 15 August.

This total 'communalization' of the services, including the police and the military, which was in a sense the concomitant of the two nation-theory and the establishment of a sovereign Pakistan, was a catastrophic decision. If government employees, with their guaranteed terms and conditions of service, felt unsafe in a Dominion in which they belonged to the minority community, how could that community feel safe and stay on under the new regime?[8] The memories of the riots in West Punjab and East Bengal were still fresh in the minds of the non-Muslim minorities; they knew that Pakistan had been created as a homeland for Muslims; they wondered if they could have a safe and honourable niche in it.

Mountbatten had taken the precaution of forming a 'neutral body' of troops, a 'boundary force' of 55,000 men under Major-General Rees to maintain law and order during the period of transition. But General Rees felt utterly helpless, when communal disturbances broke out over a wide area in the Punjab, N.W.F.P. and Sind. The problem of suppressing communal riots suddenly became more difficult than it had ever been before. During the worst riots, in Bengal and Bihar in 1946 and in the Punjab in March 1947, it had been possible to restore order within a few days, because the police and the army were composite forces recruited from all communities. There were individual acts of partisanship, but they could always be rectified. After the partition of the country and the 'communal' reshuffling of the civil and armed forces, the safeguard of a composite police and army was no longer available. When the next round of rioting started in July–August 1947, it became impossible to halt it. The Hindu and Sikh minorities in West Pakistan, and the Muslim minority in East Punjab became helpless victims of atrocities; they could not depend upon the protection of the local authorities, which came to be infected with communalism. In West Punjab even when senior Muslim officers tried to stop the persecution of the minorities, they were unable to discipline the police, which was now wholly Muslim in composition. A similar difficulty faced those who led the police force in East Punjab. Anti-social elements took full advantage of the new situation; there were orgies of looting, arson and killing. Millions of terror-stricken Hindus and Sikhs fled westwards by rail and road to India. Similarly, long convoys of Muslim refugees from East Punjab and Delhi formed to wend their weary way to Pakistan.

The communal holocaust and the mass migration of minorities were not foreseen by those who formulated, accepted, and executed the plan for the partition of the country. But they were an inevitable consequence of the communal division of the civil and military services. Three years earlier, Jinnah had declined

to heed Gandhi's plea against a total separation between the
two successor-states.[9] The Mahatma had warned that it would
bring untold misery to the minorities in both countries and
result in perpetual hatred, bitterness and wars between them.
His worst fears were tragically confirmed even while the ink on
the Mountbatten Plan had not yet quite dried.

V

Gandhi was not present at Delhi to take part in the pageantry
which was to mark the transfer of power from Britain to India
on 15 August 1947. He was in no mood to think of bands and
banners. The day for which he had longed and laboured had
come, but he felt no joy in his heart. Not only was India's
freedom being ushered in at the cost of her unity, but large
sections of the population were uneasy about their future.

Early in August 1947, Gandhi left for East Bengal, where the
Hindus of Noakhali feared a fresh wave of disturbances after the
establishment of Pakistan. On arrival at Calcutta he found the
town in the grip of communal lawlessness which had been its lot
for a year. With the exit of the Muslim League ministry and the
transfer of the majority of Muslim officials and police to Pakistan,
the tables had been turned. It seemed as if the Hindus of
Calcutta were determined to pay off old scores. Suhrawardy,
now no longer Premier, and therefore somewhat chastened, met
Gandhi and urged him to pacify Calcutta before proceeding to
Noakhali. Gandhi agreed on the condition that Suhrawardy
would stay with him under the same roof in Calcutta, and also
use his influence with Muslim opinion in East Bengal to protect
the Hindu minority.

Gandhi's choice fell upon a Muslim workman's house in
Belighata, a part of Calcutta, which was considered unsafe for
Muslims. Hardly had he moved into his new quarters, when on
13 August, a group of young Hindus staged a demonstration
against his peace mission. He explained to them how he had
been trying to end the fratricidal strife, and how hate and
violence would lead them nowhere. His words fell like gentle
rain on parched earth, and the youngmen returned to their
homes converted. Calcutta was transformed overnight. Rioting
ceased. On 14 August, the eve-of-independence was jointly

celebrated by the two communities. Hindus and Muslims collected in the streets and danced and sang together. The incubus which had pressed down upon the heart of the town since August 1946 was suddenly lifted. Three to four thousand people attended Gandhi's prayer meetings, where the flags of India and Pakistan flew together. Gandhi was pleased. 'We have drunk the poison of hatred', he said, 'and so this nectar of fraternization tastes all the sweeter'.

This cordiality had hardly lasted for a fortnight when the news of the massacres in Pakistan and the mass migrations from West Punjab caused a fresh flare-up in Calcutta. A Hindu mob raided Gandhi's residence in Belighata on 31 August; it was angry, abusive, violent; it smashed the windows and forced its way into the house. The Mahatma's words were drowned in a violent din; a brick flew past him; a *lathi* blow just missed him. Calcutta relapsed into rioting.

This was a serious setback to Gandhi's efforts for peace. His answer was the announcement of a fast from 1 September, to be broken only when peace returned to Calcutta. 'What my word in person could not do', he said, 'my fast may'. The announcement electrified the town; the Muslims were moved, the Hindus shamed. Not even the hooligans of Calcutta could bear the thought of having the Mahatma's blood on their conscience; truck-loads of contraband arms were voluntarily surrendered by the communal underground. The leaders of all communities pledged themselves to peace and begged Gandhi to break the fast. Gandhi consented, but with the warning that if the pledge was not honoured he would embark on an irrevocable fast.

The Calcutta fast was universally acclaimed as a miracle; in the oft-quoted words of the correspondent of London *Times*, it did what several divisions of troops could not have done. Henceforth Calcutta and Bengal were to remain calm; the fever of communal strife had subsided.

The finest tribute to Gandhi's work in Calcutta was paid by Mountbatten in a telegram on 26 August: 'My dear Gandhiji, in the Punjab we have 55 thousand soldiers and large-scale rioting on our hands. In Bengal our forces consist of one man and there is no rioting. As a serving officer, as well as an administrator may I be allowed to pay my tribute to the One Man Boundary Force'.[10]

VI

The sum of human misery involved in the movement of six million Hindus and Sikhs from West Punjab to East Punjab, and of an equal number of Muslims in the opposite direction was appalling. The danger, however, was that as the refugees with their tales of woe continued to pour in, violence might spread. Indeed, this was exactly what happened in Delhi. When Gandhi arrived there in September 1947 he found the capital of India paralyzed by one of the worst communal riots in its long history. He felt there was no point in his proceeding to the Punjab when Delhi was aflame.

The Government of India had taken prompt and energetic action. Prime Minister Nehru had declared that violence would be suppressed sternly; an emergency committee of the cabinet had been formed and troops had been moved into the town. But Gandhi was not content with a peace imposed by the police and the military; violence had to be purged from the hearts of the people. It was an uphill task. Delhi had a number of refugee camps, some of which housed Hindus and Sikhs from West Pakistan, while others sheltered Muslims fleeing from Delhi for a passage across the border. The Hindu and Sikh refugees were in a difficult mood. Many of them, uprooted from their homes, lands and occupations, were going through the unfamiliar pangs of poverty; some had been bereaved in the riots, and all were bitter. They could not understand the Mahatma's advice to 'forget and forgive' and to bear no malice in their hearts towards those at whose hands they had suffered. They even blamed him for the division of India; his non-violence, they said, had been outclassed by violence.

The tales of woe Gandhi heard burnt themselves into his soul, but he did not falter in his conviction that only non-violence could end this spiral of hate and violence. In his prayer speech every evening, he touched on the communal problem. He stressed the futility of retaliation. He wore himself out in an effort to re-educate the people of Delhi; he heard grievances, suggested solutions, encouraged or admonished his numerous interviewers, visited refugee camps, remained in touch with local officials. It was an exhausting and heart-breaking routine.

On 13 January 1948, Gandhi began a fast. 'My greatest fast', he wrote to one of his disciples. It was also to be his last; it was not to be broken until Delhi became peaceful. The town was ostensibly quiet; thanks to the stern measures taken by the government, the killings had stopped. But the peace for which Gandhi had been working for four and a half months was not the peace of the grave, but a peace symbolizing the reunion of hearts. Of the latter there was no sign. Muslims did not dare to move about freely in the town; reports reached Gandhi that the refugees from West Pakistan were applying subtle methods to oust local Muslims from their shops and houses. The argument that Hindus and Sikhs were equally unsafe throughout the whole of West Pakistan struck him as irrelevant.

Gandhi's fast shook the country. It compelled people to think afresh on the problem on the solution of which he had staked his life. There was a sense of urgency; something had to be done quickly to create conditions to end his fast. The Government of India paid out to Pakistan, at his instance, and as a gesture of goodwill, Rs 55 crores (£ 44 million) which were due as a share of united India's assets, but had been withheld on account of the conflict in Kashmir. On 18 January 1948, representatives of the various communities and parties in Delhi signed a pledge in Gandhi's presence that they would guarantee peace in Delhi. Before breaking the fast, the Mahatma told them, what he had told the signatories of the peace pledge at Calcutta in September 1947, that if they did not honour the pledge, he would fast unto death.

Gandhi's fast had a refreshing effect upon Pakistan; it punctured the subtle web of Muslim League propaganda which for ten years had painted him as an enemy of Islam. The tide of communal violence showed definite signs of ebbing in the sub-continent. Gandhi felt freer to make his plans for the future. He had promised the refugees from West Pakistan that he would not rest until every family had been rehabilitated in its native town or village. But he felt he could not go to Pakistan without the permission of the government of that country. Meanwhile he thought of returning to his ashram at Sevagram. His mind was switching over more and more to social and economic problems, and to the refurbishing of his non-violent technique. However, he was destined neither to go to Pakistan nor to pick up the threads of his constructive, socio-economic programme.

On the afternoon of 30 January, while he was on his way to his prayer meeting, he was shot down by a Hindu fanatic, who belonged to the school of thought which believed that Gandhi was much too soft towards Muslims and Pakistan, and had betrayed the interests of his own community and country.

VII

It is clear that Jinnah had not thought out the full implications of his two-nation theory. While a substantial portion of the Muslim population lived in the provinces he claimed for Pakistan, almost an equal number lived in the rest of India. The secession of the Muslim-majority provinces in the west and the east in 1947, far from solving the minority problem, only aggravated it. The position of the Hindu minority in Pakistan and the Muslim minority in India became immeasurably weaker than before. If it was Jinnah's object—as he professed for nearly four decades—to contribute to the solidarity of Indian Islam, he pursued a course which was to defeat this very purpose. In the event the Muslim community in the subcontinent was split in two states in 1947, and in three states after 1971. The emergence of Bangladesh, within a quarter of a century of the establishment of Pakistan, showed that religion by itself could not be a sufficient bond for nationhood. As a writer put it recently, 'the "two-nation" theory, formulated in the middle class living rooms of Uttar Pradesh was buried in the Bengali countryside'.[11] Today there are almost as many Muslims in India as in Pakistan, or in Bangladesh. And if Pakistan has no 'minority' problem it is because it has hardly any religious minorities left within its borders.

Jinnah's triumph in 1947 was the triumph of superior tactics rather than that of a sound strategy. His unswerving goal was the capture of power. However, the will and the desire for power alone would not have made him the Qaid-i-Azam. He succeeded because there was, in psychological parlance, a 'congruence that existed between his needs and characteristics and the needs of his people'.[12] 'This power-conscious man', in the words of Khalid B. Sayeed, promised to Indian Muslims, 'the political power which the Quran had promised to them and which their forbears had wielded in India'.[13] Pride in the past, and fear of the future made Indian Muslims susceptible to the cries of religion in danger.

That Jinnah was a superb tactician nobody can deny. But those who shape the destiny of nations need to be good strategists as well. He turned the conflict between the Congress and the government to good account for his aims, and in the last phase of the political tug-of-war, he was able to stall the Indian National Congress as well as the British. But he does not seem to have foreseen the long-term consequences of his campaign. The result was that he managed to achieve just the opposite of his professed aims. He had stressed the need for Muslim unity; in fact, he was destined to split Indian Muslims. The partition did not solve the communal problem; it only internationalized it. What had been a political debate between rival communities and political parties became an issue between two 'sovereign' states, which after three wars since 1947, are still debating the possibilities of a 'no-war pact'.

Jinnah had concentrated on the alleged iniquity of the Congress and the Hindu 'tyranny' during his campaign for Pakistan. The new state had hardly any guidelines from its founder, who unfortunately passed away a year after it came into existence. What was to be the political structure of the new state? What were to be its social and economic policies? The Qaid-i-Azam left no blueprint, and thirty-five years after his death, Pakistan is in the midst of an anguished struggle to seek answers to these questions.

A recent writer, in his analysis of the causes of the upheaval which accompained the partition, has argued that the 'holocaust that attended the partition and the mass migration that took place were not inherent in the partition [of India], but were a consequence of the communal division of the services'.[14] The communal division of the civil and military services was, however, inherent in Jinnah's concept of the division of the country, and his refusal to have any formal links between the two states. The causes of the disturbances which rocked the subcontinent are thus to be sought not only in the sequence of events in the summer and autumn of 1947, but in the way the seven-year-long campaign for Pakistan was waged and won.

The campaign had begun in March 1940 on a strident note, when Jinnah called for a 'homeland' for Indian Muslims in the

east and the west, to save them, after the British departure,
from 'Hindu Raj' in an independent and democratic India. He
overcame opposition within his community by appeals to religious emotion;[15] any Muslim politician who differed with him
ran the risk of being dubbed a stooge of the Hindus and a traitor
to Islam. It was on a wave of religious frenzy that the Muslim
League rode to victory in the 1946 elections.[16]

Jinnah had been initiated into politics in the early years of the
twentieth century in the modern, secular tradition of Dadabhai
Naoroji and Gokhale, and was far from being a religious fanatic.
But he was not averse from using religious passion to build up
his following and to achieve his political aims. 'In politics', he
once remarked, 'one has to play one's game as on the chess
board'. Almost till the end he kept his opponents as well as his
adherents guessing; he deliberately refrained from spelling out
the political, social and even geographical implications of
Pakistan. The very arguments on which he based his case for
the separation of Muslim-majority areas in the west and the
east from the rest of the country made the partition of the
Punjab and Bengal inevitable. It is doubtful if the Muslims of
West Bengal and East Punjab would have voted for Pakistan in
the general elections to the provincial legislatures in 1946 if the
prospect of the partition of these provinces had been brought
home to them.

The unceasing tirades against the Congress and the Hindus,
and the demand for a Muslim 'homeland' in the subcontinent
made it difficult for the non-Muslim inhabitants of the provinces
claimed for Pakistan, to believe that they could have an
honourable place in the new set-up. It is true that on 14 August
1947, in his address to the Pakistan Constituent Assembly,
Jinnah declared that there would be no discrimination between
Muslims and non-Muslims, and religious differences would
vanish in course of time. The assurance, however, came too late
to reassure the non-Muslim minorities, and too early to convince
the Muslim majority, which was justifiably elated at the establishment of an Islamic state.

The communal disturbances in August 1947 unfortunately
occurred too soon after the transfer of power; there was no time
for the purging of old hatreds. It required courage and patience
to fight against mass madness. Gandhi had foreseen this

madness and gone to Bengal well in time. In the Punjab there was no one to do a similar exercise; if a Pakistani leader had done in Lahore what Gandhi was doing in Calcutta, the course of events might have been reversed. But almost by reflex action, the League leaders reverted to their policy of putting all the blame on the Hindus; the old slanging match between the League and the Congress became a slanging match between India and Pakistan.

VIII

The Muslim League's insistence on the division of the British Indian army on a communal basis may have been a logical application of the two-nation theory and two sovereign states, but its inevitable result was the holocaust in north-western India in 1947, which led to a terrible loss of life and the migration of minorities. Were it not for the determined stand taken by Gandhi and Nehru against communal madness, its consequences in 1947 could have been even more catastrophic. It was their total commitment to secularism and religious tolerance, and their insistence that independent India did not subscribe to the two-nation theory (even after accepting the division of the country), which prevented the communal contagion from spreading beyond East Punjab and Delhi into the interior of the subcontinent.

Gandhi's influence was throughout cast against violence. His satyagraha movements had helped to sterilize political terrorism; but for him, the Indian nationalist movement might have developed into a violent struggle against the colonial power, waged with bombs and rifles, as in most other countries.

Despite British propaganda to the contrary at the time, Gandhi's efforts to keep his civil disobedience movement non-violent were largely successful in 1920–2, 1931–4 and in 1940–1. If there were violent outbreaks, they were few and far between. Gandhi knew how to stop them, if necessary by undertaking fasts. The 'Quit India' movement was a case apart; its context has been explained in the next chapter; and it needs only to be stressed that even its unregulated violence ('spontaneous revolution' as an American scholar describes it)[17] was directed not so much against British soldiers or civilians as against the

symbols of foreign rule. Gandhi was, of course, opposed to all
violence; by immediately imprisoning him, the government
prevented him from exercising his restraining influence.

No serious student of Gandhi's life and the nationalist movement can deny that Gandhi's weight was all along thrown
against all violence, and especially against communal violence.
In 1924 he undertook a 21-day fast in Delhi to stop riots. His last
two fasts in Calcutta and Delhi in 1947–8 were intended to end
the violence which the partition of the country had triggered.
His efforts met with success though they cost him his life at the
hands of a Hindu fanatic, who thought him too indulgent to
Muslims and Pakistan.

The responsibility for the violence which accompanied and
immediately followed the transfer of power cannot be fairly laid
on Gandhi. Neither the British government nor the Congress
and League leaders, who accepted the partition plan, wanted
violence. Mountbatten, who hurried the process for the transfer
of power and reduced the transition period from twelve to a
mere two-and-a half months, failed to envisage fully the possibilities of disorder. He believed he had taken enough precautions
by raising a 'Boundary Force' of 55,000 men under a British
general to keep the peace. In the event, this action proved
inadequate. The governments of the two new Dominions, even
before they were able to start functioning, were confronted with
a critical situation. Of one thing, however, there is no doubt: no
one in the Indian subcontinent did more than Gandhi to warn
against the dangers of its partition on a religious basis, or did
more to quench the flames of hatred and violence which followed it.

CHAPTER 13

Gandhi and Non-Violence

Some commentators on Gandhi have questioned the sincerity and consistency of his belief in non-violence. 'And what of his pacifism', asks a writer in the *Washington Post*, 'the quality that supposedly makes him a man for our time. Gandhi was singularly bellicose until the age of 50. Not only was he eager to kill off the Zulus, but also the Boers and all Britain's World War enemies'.[1] With a malicious pleasure some critics refer to the 'military' record of 'Sergeant-Major Gandhi' in the Zulu Rebellion, the Boer War and the First World War. Curiously, the same critics, who accuse Gandhi of 'bellicosity', cite the Quit India movement of 1942 as evidence of his purblind pacifism and pro-Fascist sympathies in the Second World War.

What is the truth in this picture of Gandhi as a war-monger, a trigger-happy Sergeant, in his youth and middle age, and as a sympathizer of the Axis Powers during the Second World War? None at all. In 1906 while Gandhi was practising as a barrister at Johannesburg, he had led—with the rank of Sergeant-Major—a group of twenty Indian stretcher-bearers to nurse Africans wounded during the operations against 'the Zulu Rebellion' in Natal; it was a mission of mercy, all the more valuable because the British soldiers and doctors were reluctant to attend on the unfortunate victims of the military expedition. Seven years earlier, in 1899 during the Boer War, Gandhi raised a 1200-strong ambulance corps from among Indian residents of Natal. On both these occasions, he had argued that since the Indian community claimed equality in rights with the Europeans in Natal and Transvaal, it must also accept equal obligations; and one of the obligations of citizenship was participation in the defence of the country.

To equate Gandhi's ambulance work with 'war-mongering'

is absurd, but it must be admitted that in these early years Gandhi's views on non-violence had not yet fully crystallized. In his immediate domestic and social circles, and even in his political work, he was talking of overcoming opposition by persuasion, and hatred by love. However, not until the end of 1906 and the enactment of the humiliating Asiatic Registration law, did he evolve satyagraha, his non-violent method of redressing social and political injustice. During the next eight years he tried this method with a measure of success on behalf of the hard-pressed Indian minority in South Africa. But he had not yet thought out all the implications of non-violence, especially in its application to conflicts between nation-states.

When the First World War broke out, Gandhi was on his way to India from South Africa via London. Immediately after arrival in England, he conferred with the Indian residents, most of whom were students. He gave them the same advice as he had given to his compatriots in Natal and Transvaal; if they claimed equal rights as citizens of the British empire, they must do their bit for Britain, their adopted country, in its hour of trial. He took the initiative in organizing an Indian Ambulance Corps in England, and would himself have served in it in the battle-fronts of Europe, if an attack of pleurisy had not compelled him to leave for India in December 1914.

By 1914 Gandhi's views on non-violence had reached the stage where it was unthinkable for him personally to engage in killing and war, but he recognized that most of his countrymen did not share this attitude. Indeed, Indian political leaders, 'moderate' as well as 'extremist', were unanimous that the people of India should support the British cause against the Germans, but only for a price—the promise of home rule after the war. Gandhi was almost alone in rejecting the idea of a political bargain with the British; he cherished the hope that in return for unconditional support, a grateful and victorious Britain would give India her due when the war was over.

The First World War created a moral dilemma for Gandhi. His own ideas on non-violence had advanced to the point that he could not personally participate in any act of violence; the utmost he could do was to nurse the wounded. While he was personally opposed to violence and to war, those who looked up to him for guidance were not. His faith in the British empire and in the possibility of India attaining within it an autonomous status similar to that of Canada or Australia was undimmed. He argued that since the people of India claimed equal rights as citizens of the empire, they had also to accept the duties of this status in times of war. The Indians whom Gandhi led in ambulance units in the battle-fields of South Africa or whom he exhorted to join the British Indian army in the First World War did not believe in non-violence. It was not repugnance to violence but indifference or cowardice which held them back from participating in the war. And since the people of India were not ready for non-violent resistance, (Gandhi argued) it was their duty to support Britain in her war-effort. So intense, however, was Gandhi's hatred of all violence and war, that it was not without much heart-searching and inner anguish that he reached this conclusion. To a colleague who had expressed his surprise at Gandhi's offer to associate himself with the war even for ambulance work he replied: 'I myself could not shoot, but could nurse the wounded. I might even get Germans to nurse. I could nurse them without any partisan spirit. That would be no violation of the spirit of compassion then'.[2]

During the two decades, which spanned the First and the Second World Wars, Gandhi's belief in the potentialities of non-violence grew with greater reflection and experience. Such was the emphasis which he began to place on non-violence that it seemed that the means were more important to him than the goal. In November 1931 he went so far as to say: 'And I would like to repeat to the world times without number, that I will not purchase my country's freedom, at the cost of non-violence. My marriage to non-violence is such an absolute thing that I would rather commit suicide than be deflected from my position'.

Because of his 'absolute' commitment to non-violence, the Second World War created a situation for Gandhi which was in some ways even more difficult than the one he had faced in the 1914 war. He had simultaneously to play the role of the leader of the nationalist movement in India and the prophet of non-violence in the war-torn world; this brought out two independent and occasionally contradictory strands in his position. He had publicly hailed Nehru as his 'guide' on international affairs. At Nehru's instance, the Indian National Congress had denounced every act of aggression by the fascist powers in Manchuria,

Abyssinia, Spain and Czechoslovakia, and taken the Western powers to task for their policy of 'appeasement' towards the dictators. Gandhi's dislike of Hitler and Mussolini was as intense as Nehru's. He defined Hitlerism as a 'naked ruthless force reduced to an exact science worked with scientific precision', and Nazism and Fascism 'as symptoms of a deep-seated disease—the cult of violence'.

As the threat of war grew in the late 1930s and the forces of violence gathered momentum, Gandhi re-asserted his faith in the efficacy of non-violence. He felt more strongly than ever that at that moment of crisis in world history he had a message for India, and that India had a message for bewildered humanity. Through the pages of his weekly paper, the *Harijan*, he expounded his non-violent approach to political tyranny and military aggression. He advised the weaker nations to defend themselves not by seeking protection from better armed states, nor by increasing their own fighting potential, but by non-violent resistance to the aggressor. A non-violent Abyssinia, he argued, needed no arms and no succour from the League of Nations; if every Abyssinian man, woman and child refused cooperation with the Italians, willing or forced, the latter would have to walk to victory over the dead bodies of their victims and to occupy the country without the people.

Gandhi was obviously making a heavy overdraft upon human endurance. It required supreme courage for a whole people to die to the last man, woman and child, rather than surrender to the enemy. Non-violent resistance was, however, not a soft doctrine—a convenient refuge from a dangerous situation; nor was it an offer on a platter to the dictators of what they plotted to wrest by force.

Gandhi was aware of the apotheosis of violence which Nazi and Fascist regimes represented, but he did not accept that Hitler and Mussolini were beyond redemption. A fundamental assumption in his philosophy was that human nature in essence was one and must ultimately respond to love. 'If the enemy realized', wrote Gandhi, 'that you have not the remotest thought in your mind of raising your hand against him even for the sake of your life, he will lack the zest to kill you. Every hunter has had this experience. No one had heard of anyone hunting cows'.

Thus at an early stage in the Second World War Gandhi's

own position was anchored to his pacifism. It soon became clear that few of his colleagues shared his faith in the efficacy of non-violence in armed conflicts. Nehru, Azad, Rajagopalachari, and indeed the majority of the Congress leaders, did not view the war as an occasion for testing the potentialities of non-violence; the really important point was whether the monstrous war-machine built by Hitler could be destroyed before it enslaved mankind. The Indian National Congress, as Nehru put it, 'had accepted the principle and practices of non-violence in its application to the struggle for freedom [against the British]. At no time had it gone beyond that position, or applied the principle to defence from external aggression or internal disorder'.

The differences between Gandhi and his colleagues would have sharply come into focus, if the British government had not been short-sighted enough to freeze the constitutional issue for the duration of the war. So long as there was no prospect of an effective Congress participation in the central government, the question whether India's support of the Allied cause was to be moral (as Gandhi advocated) or military (as Nehru proposed), remained purely academic. There were two occasions on which the vicissitudes of war seemed to bring a rapprochement between the Congress and the government within the realm of practical politics, in 1940 after the French collapse, and in 1941–2 after the Japanese advance in Southeast Asia. On both these occasions Gandhi found that the majority of his colleagues were ready to switch to a whole-hearted participation in the Allied war effort in return for a reciprocal gesture by the British government. It is significant that in April 1942 the Congress leaders' parleys with Sir Stafford Cripps broke down not on the issue of violence versus non-violence, but on the composition and powers of a provisional national government for the effective prosecution of war.

For nearly three years after the outbreak of the war Gandhi successfully contained the frustration of nationalist India at the lack of an adequate response from the British government. He tried hard to balance his passion for Indian freedom with his desire not to embarrass the government during the war. In 1940–1, he conducted an 'individual' civil disobedience movement, as a symbolic protest, which (despite the imprisonment of nearly 30,000 persons) was designed to cause the least dislocation to the war-effort. Paradoxically, even the 'Quit India' movement, which Gandhi contemplated after the failure of the Cripps Mission, was intended by him to strengthen the forces of resistance against the Japanese, who were advancing all along the line in Southeast Asia. Gandhi yielded to the pleas of Nehru (whose mind was full of thoughts of citizen armies, home guards and guerilla warfare to beat off the Japanese invaders) that, after the British power from India was withdrawn, Allied forces should continue to use India as a base against the Fascist powers.

In the summer of 1942 Gandhi's hand was on the pulse of the people. He had observed that their mood in the face of the Japanese peril was not one of resolute defiance, but of panic, frustration and helplessness. Gandhi felt that if India was not to go the way of Malaya and Burma, where the people had put up little resistance and the British forces had withdrawn or been annihilated, something had to be done and done quickly. He declared that only an immediate declaration of Indian independence by the British government could give the people of India a stake in the defence of their country. As he told Generalissimo Chiang Kai-shek, the British had effected

> withdrawals from Malaya, Singapore and Burma . . . . We must learn the lesson from these tragic events and prevent by all means at our disposal a repetition of what befell these unfortunate countries. But unless we are free we can do nothing to prevent it, and the same process might well occur again, crippling India and China disastrously. I do not want a repetition of this tragic tale of woe.[3]

In this line of thinking Gandhi had been influenced by the feeling that the British in India were losing their nerve. He had seen reports of a broadcast over the All India Radio by Major-General Molesworth in February 1942, in which he had said that India's eastern coastline was some two thousand miles in length, and it was not easy to locate a raider on so vast a sea board. Speaking to the Rotary Club of Delhi the General said:

> Everybody in India is asking what are we going to do to keep the Japanese out. From the point of view of the army, in this enormous battle front we shall hold vital places which it is necessary to hold in order to make India safe, but we cannot hold every one. Therefore

what is to be done for the rest of India where we are unable to put troops or air or naval air forces? We cannot arm all. On the other hand, we can do a great deal to educate the masses to give the Japanese a great deal of trouble. This must be done by the civil people like you. The army cannot do it. The people can work in bands and give trouble and delay and destroy invasion. It may be there is no proper lead from the top and no proper leadership down below. Still, I feel the Japanese invasion can be beaten, if we educate the people on the lines of 'They shall not pass'. Psychologically it can only be done by the intelligentsia, working definitely shoulder to shoulder to work up the peasant.[4]

This indeed was Gandhi's aim in the summer of 1942, when he asked the British to transfer power to Indian hands to let the people defend their own country. Some months earlier, he had sent his English disciple, Mirabehn (Miss Slade), to Orissa to prepare the people for a non-violent resistance to the Japanese if they managed to land on the eastern coast.

Remember, [he told her] that our attitude is that of complete non-cooperation with the Japanese army, therefore, we may not help them in any way nor may we profit by any dealings with them. . . . If, however, the people have not the courage to resist . . . . One thing they [the people] should never do—to yield willing submission to the Japanese. That will be a cowardly act, and unworthy of freedom-loving people. They must not escape from one fire to fall into another and probably more terrible.[5]

Clearly, if the Axis Powers had any collaborators in India, actual or potential, Gandhi was not one of them. There is no doubt that if in August 1942 he had not been arrested, his weight would have been thrown against violent outbreaks. He knew how to bring unruly mobs to order; when appeals failed, he could bring them back to sanity by undertaking a fast.

The Government of India headed by Linlithgow, and backed by Prime Minister Churchill, acted in accordance with the view common among British administrators, that the best way of crushing Gandhi's movements was to deliver telling blows at the initial stage. In 1942 the government struck before Gandhi had a chance to launch his movement. For a few months India was caught in the vicious circle of popular terrorism and official counter-terrorism. Linlithgow, the Viceroy, who had conducted the sternest repression against the nationalist movement in

Indian history, persuaded himself that he had won a decisive victory over Gandhi. And yet two years later, his successor, Lord Wavell, wrote to Prime Minister Churchill:

> There remains a deep sense of frustration and discontent amongst practically all educated Indians, which renders the present arrangement for government insecure and impermanent . . . . The present Government of India cannot continue indefinitely, or even for long. If our aim is to retain India as a willing member of the British Commonwealth, we must make some imaginative and constructive move without delay.[6]

The British government and the Government of India used the massive resources of their war publicity machines to paint Gandhi and the Congress as 'Quislings' and saboteurs of the Allied struggle against the Axis Powers. This propaganda held the field for some time, but not for long. 'It is sheer nonsense', Field Marshal Smuts told a press conference in London in November 1942, 'to talk of Mahatma Gandhi as a fifth columnist. He is a great man. He is one of the great men of the world'.

Forty years after Smuts spoke and with the enormous documentation of that period which is available in official and non-official sources, the reiteration of the charge that Gandhi was pro-Axis, or pro-Japanese during the Second World War can only be attributed to ignorance of the facts or an unreasoning prejudice.

CHAPTER 14

Man versus Machine

Several critics who recognize Gandhi's historic role as the leader of a revolutionary movement against imperialism find his social outlook reactionary. They cite *Hind Swaraj*, a pamphlet written by Gandhi in 1909, as proof of his 'back-to-nature' philosophy—a nostalgic throw-back to a primitive, pre-modern economy.[1]

The Government of India proscribed *Hind Swaraj* for its strictures on British rule and the advocacy of non-violent resistance. But it was his denunciation of Western civilization, especially of industrialism, which disconcerted the Indian intelligentsia, who had taken their political as well as economic models from the West.

Gandhi's anti-Western stance in *Hind Swaraj* may have been partly a reaction to Western-educated Indians' proclivity to 'indiscriminate and thoughtless imitation on the assumption that Asiatics are only fit to copy everything that comes from the West'. But the fact remains that Gandhi took an extreme position on the use of machinery in *Hind Swaraj*; it seems to have stemmed from an ascetic streak in his own character, and was strengthened by his study of the nineteenth-century Christian moralists— Tolstoy, Carlyle, Ruskin, Carpenter and others—who had dwelt on the seamy side of the industrial revolution in Europe. But there was a specific Indian context in which industrialism became anathema to Gandhi. He had wept when he first read in R. C. Dutt's *Economic History of India*, how thriving village crafts and industries had been destroyed under the rule of the East India Company in the interest of British manufacturers. What pained him more than anything else was that the centre of gravity had shifted from seven hundred thousand villages, where the vast majority of the population lived, to a few cities

dominated by a parasitic class of brokers between the colonial
rulers and the Indian people—the landlords, the millowners,
the moneyed men, the professional classes and the government
servants. 'The half a dozen modern cities', Gandhi lamented,
'are an excrescence and serve at the present moment the evil
purpose of drawing the life-blood of the villages'. The pressure
on the land had grown; alternative occupations were practically
non-existent, millions of landless labourers had no gainful
employment at all, and even the farmers who worked on the
land were under-employed for several months in the year.
Urban industrialization, rural de-industrialization, widespread
unemployment and massive poverty, especially in the villages,
were the characteristic features of the Indian economy.

II

After his return to India, and with closer knowledge of the
condition of the country, Gandhi's economic thought outgrew
the uncompromising vehemence of *Hind Swaraj* and he came to
adopt a more flexible and pragmatic position on the use of
machinery.

> In the sparsely populated United States machinery is obviously
> necessary. But in India there are millions and millions of people
> who are unemployed or under-employed. Mechanization is good,
> when the hands are too few for the work intended to be accom-
> plished. It is an evil when there are more hands than are required
> for the work, as is the case in India.[2]

He welcomed the prospect of rural electrification and the
introduction of tools and instruments in village crafts which
could lighten the burden of work and fatigue. He did not,
however, support technological innovation for its own sake;
mechanization was acceptable to him only if it did not displace
useful labour, and did not lead to the concentration of production
and distribution in a few hands. Where machinery was essential,
he was all for establishment of factories in which workers were
assured not only of a living wage, but of a task which was not
mere drudgery.

The fundamental problem of the Indian economy, as Gandhi
saw it, was chronic unemployment and under-employment in

the villages. 'The problem with us', he wrote, 'is not to find a leisure for teeming millions inhabiting our country. The problem is how to utilize their idle hours which are equal to the working days of six months in the year. Dead machinery must not be pitted against the millions of living machines represented by the villagers scattered in the seven hundred thousand villages of India. Machinery to be well-used has to help and ease human effort.'[3]

Gandhi's attitude to mechanization was thus not based on blind prejudice; he was not an Indian Luddite. His eyes were riveted on the long-suffering population of the villages of the Indian subcontinent, which had suffered neglect for centuries. His thinking had a pronounced rural bias. He looked upon urbanization as an evil, and the cities as the agents of exploitation, which had 'sapped the lifeblood of the villages'. Urban-based crafts, especially those catering to luxury tastes and export markets, did not interest him. Nor did he feel much sympathy for the migrants from the villages who eked out a precarious living through trade or personal service in large cities; he felt they should never have left their villages. The common impression that Gandhi was opposed in principle to technology is erroneous; he only asked for an appropriate technology.

Jawaharlal Nehru, who had once been a critic of Gandhi's stance on mechanization, learnt to see the rationale behind it. Referring to the large experimental mechanized farm at Suratgarh in Rajasthan, Nehru remarked:

A hundred Suratgarhs would naturally multiply the production of one Suratgarh a hundred times, but what you forget is the vast human element involved in any consideration of rural India. We don't lack people. They constitute our biggest machine or lever or whatever you like to call it. As Gandhiji used to stress to us all the time: You talk about the machine, well, I am not against the machine, he would say, but we happen to have thirty crores (three hundred million) machines in India. Why should we not use them? They are the human beings who work. Peasants with tremendous capacity for work. Now you may get a better machine per man or hundred men or over a thousand men, but you are wasting thirty crores, or twenty crores or ten crores of machines, and they are not merely machines, they are human beings, who have to be fed, looked after . . . . So coming to the point, if we put Suratgarhs all over the place, what is one to do with our labour potential?[4]

What was true of agriculture was truer of industry. India could not brush mechanization aside; but it had to be adopted discriminately, if the large and growing labour force was not to swell the ranks of the unemployed. Mere growth of G.N.P. would avail the country little, if millions of men remained in enforced idleness and destitution. 'I do visualise', Gandhi wrote, 'electricity, ship-building, iron works, machine-making and the like existing side by side with village handicrafts. But the order of dependence will be reversed. Hitherto the industrialization has been so planned as to destroy the villages and village crafts. In the State of the future, it will subserve the villages and their crafts'.

It was not Gandhi's habit to preach what he did not practise. In 1936 he decided to settle in a village. His choice fell upon a small village, Segaon near Wardha in central India, which had a population of six hundred, but was devoid of such basic amenities as a road, a shop and a post office. Here, on land owned by his friend and disciple, Jamnalal Bajaj, Gandhi occupied a one-room hut. When Dr John Mott interviewed him in 1937, Gandhi's was the solitary hut, but before long a colony of mud and bamboo houses grew up, and Segaon, renamed Sevagram, became the centre of Gandhi's scheme of village welfare. A number of institutions grew up in and around Sevagram. The All-India Village Industries Association supported and developed such industries as could easily be fostered in the villages, required little capital and did not need help from outside the village. The Association set up a school for training village workers and published a periodical. Among other organizations were those which sought to improve the breed of the cows and the system of school education.

There was hardly an aspect of village life—whether it was housing, sanitation, medical aid, fertilizers, cattle care or marketing—which did not engage Gandhi's attention. One of the problems, to which he gave much thought, was nutrition. He discovered with something of a shock that, apart from their poverty, food habits of the people in the villages were responsible for their under-nourishment. The deficiency in vitamins was inexcusable when green leaves were available for the picking. 'As a practised cook', Gandhi wrote on methods of cooking which did not destroy the nutritive value of foods. He appealed

to Indian scientists to carry out research on Indian diets. 'It is
for you', he told them, 'to make these experiments. Don't say
off-hand that Bengalis need half a pound of rice everyday and
must digest half a pound. Devise a scientifically perfect diet for
them. Determine the quality of starch required for an average
human constitution. I would not be satisfied until I have been
able to add some milk fat and greens to the diet of our common
village folk. I want chemists who would starve in order to find
an ideal diet for our common village folk. Unfortunately, our
doctors have never approached the question from the humani-
tarian standpoint, at any rate from the poor man's standpoint'.

Gandhi did not consider human welfare only in material
terms. Nor did he accept that the test of civilization was endless
multiplication of wants. At the same time, he did not idealize
poverty. Deeply religious as he was, he remarked that 'to a
people famishing and idle, the only acceptable form of God that
can dare appear is work and promise of food as wages'. Nevertheless, he put first things first: food, clothing, shelter, health
care, and education for the masses had to take precedence over
luxury goods such as washing machines and motor cars. He set
up the ideal of *voluntary poverty* before the Indian elite as 'the
concrete expression of identification with the cause of *daridra-
narayana* [the poor]'. In other words, 'the non-material motivation
had to be the driving force of any genuine programme of national
development'.[5]

The revival and revitalization of India's villages was Gandhi's
constant concern: 'We must mentally go back to the villages,
and treat them as our pattern, instead of putting up the city life
before them for imitation'. The cities, he said, were capable of
taking care of themselves. 'It is the villages we have to turn to.
We have to disabuse them of their prejudices, their superstition,
their narrow outlook, and we can do so in no other manner than
that of staying amongst them and sharing their joys and sorrows
and spreading education and intelligent information among
them.'

Living in a village, constantly thinking about the problems of
the village, Gandhi was seeking solutions with the human and
material resources of the village. He talked of 'village swaraj'
(village self-government) which would ensure that each village
was self-sufficient for its vital requirements, growing its own

food and its own cotton for its cloth, with its own school, theatre and public hall, and its own local officials supervised by a locally elected panchayat.

III

It must be admitted that Gandhi's views on the 'self-sufficiency of the village' and on limited industrialization did not commend themselves to the Indian intelligentsia, not even to most of his own colleagues in the Congress Party. They saw no alternative to India treading the road traversed by Europe, America and Japan. Indeed, they felt India had to accelerate the pace to make up for lost time. They considered a strong and diversified industrial base imperative for India if she was to fit into the world as it was in the middle of the twentieth century.

Independent India under Nehru did not adopt the Gandhian model of economic development. But the successive Five-Year Plans have recognized the value of some of Gandhi's ideas, and have included programmes for the uplift of rural India, cottage industries and village self-government. But the basic structure of the plans was based on the concept of 'modernization'— large-scale industrialization.

Economists may have laughed at Gandhi's ideas in his lifetime; they do so no longer.[6] Their conceit has taken a heavy battering; their calculations have gone awry, and they may now be in a more chastened mood to benefit from some of Gandhi's insights. Many of them had hoped that industrialization would trigger in the newly liberated countries of Asia and Africa processes of social change, such as Europe and America had witnessed in the eighteenth and nineteenth centuries. However, the results have not been quite what they had expected them to be. It is true that there has been a sizeable expansion of agricultural and industrial production in some developing countries, including India, but the gap between the rich and the poor, the urban and the rural, the educated and the illiterate has been widening. Clearly, there are dangers of social unrest, conflict and violence in a situation in which growing production goes hand in hand with increasing unemployment and poverty in the countryside.

Gandhi was not an economist, but he intuitively stumbled upon some basic truths about the socio-economic conditions in

his own country, which may also be relevant to several other
Third World countries. In the first place, he recognized the
predominance of the self-employed producer, agriculturist and
artisan, engaged in producing for his basic requirements and
not for the pursuit of wealth for its own sake. These small
producers are a social category, fundamentally different from
the mediaeval surfs as well as the modern proletariat of the
Marxist analysis. Nor do these small, self-employed producers,
working and living within the constraints of community life in
the village, correspond to the individual-based capitalist model,
so beloved of the Western liberal-rationalist school. The disintegration of the small peasant and the artisan economy, and
the growth of large-scale enterprises, based on modern technology, form a common ground between the advocates of the
capitalist and the communist models of development. But
Gandhi sensed the difficulties and dangers of alienating millions
of small producers, who formed the bulk of the population, from
the means of production. His perception that 'the participation
of this vast force in economic development calls for a new
approach and exploration outside the bounds of Western or
Soviet models has been fully borne out by recent Indian
experience'.[7]

Secondly, Gandhi saw that poverty in India was primarily a
consequence of a neglected rural economy and enforced unemployment. This unemployment was not associated—as in
industrialized countries—with a deficiency of aggregate demand;
it was structural in nature and could only be tackled by the
restructuring of the economy. Gandhi suggested dispersal of
industries in the villages, and the creation of viable rural
economies. He also challenged some of the basic postulates of
the economists. He did not assess economic progress merely in
terms of per capita income. His concept of economic progress
was a composite one, partly economic, partly moral and partly
spiritual.[8] For him there could be no ethically neutral economics.
If a lower rate of economic growth was the price to be paid for a
wider diffusion of technology and productive capacity and for
greater social justice and lesser depredation of environment,
Gandhi would have gladly paid it.

The Gandhian concept of development thus relates to man as
a whole, not just to the 'economic man'; it seeks to avoid

distortions in the relationship between man and his environment, between man and machine, between labour and capital, and between village and town. Gandhi's economic thinking was mainly done for India—and indirectly for other Third World countries, which were struggling to free themselves from colonial rule. But some of his insights can now be seen to be especially relevant to the malaise that afflicts the developed world today. Apart from the environmental degradation, which is the by-product of a runaway technology, there is the social fragmentation which breaks up families and communities, fosters crime and corruption, creates a vacuum in all forms of authority, and promotes a manipulative form of authoritarianism, rooted not only in the transitional processes of production, but in a closer integration between Big Business and Big Government.

Gandhi had warned against the technological determinism in which the world seems to have already landed itself. He had no use for technological innovations which dehumanized man, alienated him from his work or from his fellow workers, and created a civilization of human robots in which one group of men could easily manipulate others.

Gandhi's warnings against the unrestricted growth of the machine civilization, sounded well before the First World War, were laughed out of court. But in 1949, a year after Gandhi's death, George Orwell published his celebrated novel *1984*. It was a grim fantasy, which threatens to turn out to be a brilliant forecast. Some of Orwell's prognostications in the scientific, social and political spheres have already been realized. Teams of experts are already planning the logistics of future wars; there is a 'siege mentality', beginnings of a political hysteria, of unbridled terrorism, and counter-terrorism. The nemesis of the 'machine civilization' may be closer at hand than many of us imagine.

CHAPTER 15

A Reactionary?

The eighteen accused in the Meerut Conspiracy Case, who included some of the founding fathers of the Communist Party of India, in their long statement before the court declared that Gandhi's civil disobedience campaigns were a means of 'sabotaging revolutionary movements', that the Indian National Congress under his leadership shied away from violence, as it did not want to overthrow foreign rule, that Gandhi was really working for a compromise with British imperialism in the interests of the Indian bourgeoisie. This statement was in accord with the thesis propounded to the Second Communist International in 1920 by M. N. Roy;[1] it continued to colour the thinking of Indian communists for a quarter of a century; it prevented them even from recognizing the fact of Indian independence for some years after 1947. It is not surprising that Gandhi figures in communist—and even in some of the socialist writings of the period—not only as a half-hearted rebel, but as a defender of the status quo[2] and the protector of the vested interests of the Indian princes, the landlords and the capitalists. Curiously enough this image of Gandhi has been recently promoted by a section of the ultra-conservative capitalist press in the West. 'Gandhi was . . . in the highest degree reactionary', we are told, 'permitting in India no change in the relationship between the feudal lord and his peasants or servants, the rich and the poor'.[3]

It is an untenable thesis, but it acquired some plausibility from Gandhi's unorthodox approach to the phenomena of social change. From the days of *Hind Swaraj*, he had been advocating the reordering of social relationships, but without resort to violence. His approach to social transformation was diametrically opposed to that of the Marxists. He read Karl Marx's *Das Kapital* rather late in life, in his seventy-fifth year. He admired Marx's vision and dynamism and his identification 'with the poor, oppressed toilers of the world', and would have agreed with him that philosophers have interpreted the world in various ways; the point, however, is to change it. But he rejected much of the Marxist doctrine. He did not accept that economic factors were the source of all the evils in the world, that wars were necessarily caused by economic factors, that the state is wholly evil under a capitalist system, and that it would automatically wither away when state socialism emerged through a violent revolution. He did not think that class struggle was inevitable; he affirmed that his non-violent technique could be invoked for social transformation as well as for anti-colonial struggles.

When Gandhi talked of basing socialism and communism on non-violence, it seemed to his critics that he was being totally unrealistic. Was it not wishful thinking to exhort the rulers of princely states in India to convert themselves from despots into trustees of the people's welfare, to expect landlords voluntarily to give a new deal to their tenants, or to urge the capitalists to place their responsibilities to society above the profit motive?

Gandhi was the target of much criticism and even ridicule for his 'utopian' beliefs. What his critics failed to see was that while he was dead earnest about making drastic changes in the existing social relationships, he wanted to effect them only at the opportune moment, and in a manner which accorded with his non-violent strategy.

Gandhi had good reasons to be cautious in raising the 'social question' in the early twenties. The launching of a non-violent mass movement against the British Raj in 1921 was itself a tremendous step, fraught with great risks. The campaigns he had led in South Africa had involved a few thousand Indians in a limited area whom he could personally guide. In India the scale of the campaign was continental, the numbers involved directly and indirectly were in millions. Gandhi's constant concern was how to arouse these millions, and yet to prevent his movement from dissolving into disorder and anarchy. He never forgot the terrible sequel in the Punjab in April 1919 soon after he had launched the Rowlatt Bills satyagraha. All his energies were, therefore, directed to keeping a firm rein on the movement. He deliberately decided not to induct the industrial workers into his campaign; without adequate training they were much too prone to lose their heads. He advised the mill workers not to absent themselves without permission from their employers, if they wished to join any satyagraha demonstration. He would not permit the peasants to withhold rent from the landlords. He excluded the despotic princely states from his civil disobedience campaigns. All these self-denying ordinances baffled and infuriated Gandhi's radical colleagues, who protested that he was throwing away valuable opportunities of widening the anti-imperialist front. They chafed under the restrictions imposed by him. Why not call out the industrial workers in the streets? Why not launch a no-rent and no-tax campaign simultaneously in the countryside? Why not rouse the subjects of the Indian princes against autocracy and oppression? Why not synchronize the assault on the privileged classes in India with the battle against foreign rule?

The critics who asked these questions could not see that the basic strategy of a non-violent struggle must necessarily be different from that of a violent one. For Gandhi it was not a question of capturing a particular outpost by superior force, or of overwhelming the enemy by sheer numbers. The purpose of satyagraha was to generate those processes of introspection and rethinking which would make it possible to arrive at a readjustment of relationships, and all this had to be done without generating hatred and violence. For Gandhi non-violence was the central issue; on this he would accept no compromise. 'I would welcome', he said, 'even utter failure with non-violence unimpaired, rather than depart from it by a hair's breadth to achieve a doubtful success'. It was because of his supreme anxiety to keep the movement firmly under control that he invariably began his campaigns cautiously, and only gradually extended them in range and intensity.

II

'An able general', wrote Gandhi, 'always gives battle in his own time on the ground of his choice'.[4] In retrospect it seems that he deliberately did not open the fissures in Indian society while the main battle against the British Raj was in progress. He was criticized for his policy of non-intervention in the Indian states.

But Gandhi realized that the people of the states had little experience of political agitation, and there was a great danger of processions and meetings ending up in a vicious chain of popular violence and official repression. In 1931, when an American journalist, William Shirer, asked him why he had not organized the subjects of the Indian states against their 'princely tyrants', Gandhi told him that his struggle was primarily directed against British rule; when that rule came to an end, and India became self-governing, 'the pampered princes would have to fall in line. They would no longer have the British around to prop up their shaky thrones'.[5] Sixteen years later, when the transfer of power came, things happened exactly as Gandhi had foreseen; the princes, without the imperial power to uphold them, had no legs to stand on; their territories were integrated into the Indian Union without much fuss, and they were turned overnight into pensioners of the Indian Republic.

As for landlords and tenants, Gandhi argued that there was no irreconcilable antagonism between them. He acknowledged that there was much exploitation of the tenants and industrial workers, but this exploitation could not be removed simply by the liquidation of landlords and millowners; what was needed was the removal of the ignorance of the victims of exploitation. No exploitation was possible, Gandhi said, without the willing or forced cooperation of the exploited. 'The moment the cultivators of the soil realize their power', Gandhi wrote, 'the zamindari [landlordism] evil will be sterilized. What can the poor zamindar do when the tenants say they will simply not work the land unless they are paid enough to feed and clothe and educate themselves and their children in a decent manner? . . . If the toilers intelligently combine, they will become an irresistible power'.[6]

On the landlord–tenant relationship Gandhi's views seemed to harden progressively. 'I do not want to destroy the zamindar', he wrote in 1936, 'but neither do I feel that the zamindar is inevitable'.[7] At first he clung to the hope that it might be possible to regulate the relations between landlords and tenants on a new basis. By 1937 he was less optimistic and was affirming that 'land and all property is his who will work it'.[8] Five years later, he was even visualizing a situation in which the peasants might refuse to pay taxes and seize the land. He told Louis

Fischer, the American journalist, who questioned him on this subject on the eve of the Quit India movement, that the 'peasants will stop paying taxes; they will make salt despite official prohibition . . . . Their next step will be to seize the land'. 'With violence?' Fischer asked. 'There may be violence', Gandhi said, 'but, then again, the landlords may cooperate'. 'You are an optimist', said Fischer. Gandhi said: 'They might cooperate by fleeing'. 'Or they [the landlords] might organize violent resistance', Fischer put in. 'There may be fifteen days of chaos', Gandhi speculated, 'but I think we could soon bring that under control'.[9]

There was no doubt in Gandhi's mind about his social priorities. He said: 'The *kisan* or peasant comes first. He is the salt of the earth which belongs or should belong to him, not to the absentee landlord. But in a non-violent way, the labourer cannot forcibly eject the absentee landlord. He has so to work as to make it impossible for the landlord to exploit him.'[10]

There is no doubt that during the twenties and thirties Gandhi deliberately opposed militant action designed to keep the peasantry in perpetual excitement, and to raise hopes which could not be fulfilled without a violent conflict. Instead, through his 'constructive programme', he sought to increase the peasant's economic viability, strengthen his will to be efficient, to teach him the advantages of organized action and to fight any exploiter, whether it was the landlord, the moneylender or a petty official. He suggested cooperative farming of holdings which had been sliced and fragmented by the inexorable operation of the laws of inheritance. 'Does it not stand to reason', he asked, 'that it is far better for a hundred families in a village to cultivate their lands collectively and divide the income therefrom than to divide the land anyhow into a hundred parts? And what applies to land applies to cattle'.[11]

We must remember that the first steps towards the abolition of landlordism in India were taken before the Second World War, while the Congress ministries were in office, and their policies were being supervised by the Congress High Command with Gandhi's approval. The process received an impetus after the attainment of independence. The land legislation broke the power of the feudal landlords, and established the rights to the land of the better-off tenants, though they did not materially improve the position of the intermediary tenants nor strictly enforce ceilings on land.[12] If Gandhi had lived a few years longer, his weight would beyond doubt have been thrown in favour of the landless agriculturist and labourer, and the land reform legislation in India would have had more teeth in it.

III

Gandhi had no illusion about the motivation of the Indian capitalists. The common impression—which the British helped to spread—that Gandhi's political movements were largely financed by the capitalists is erroneous. When Gandhi launched his non-cooperation movement against the British in 1920, the Indian millowners almost as a class opposed him. An 'Anti-non-cooperation Society' came up in Bombay in 1920 with Purshotamdas Thakurdas and Chimanlal Setalvad as secretaries; its financiers included the Tatas. This society sought to combat non-cooperation through 'counter-propaganda', and worked in close cooperation with the Moderate leaders who were opposing Gandhi. It is significant that not a single industrialist signed the satyagraha pledge in March–April 1919, and with a few exceptions (such as those of Umar Sobhani and A. D. Godrej) they did not contribute anything to the Tilak Swaraj Fund. Gandhi treated the industrialists—as everybody else—with courtesy, but he had no illusions about them. In an 'open letter' published in July 1921, he told them that the merchants whom he was asking to boycott the sale of foreign cloth were sure that the Indian millowners would exploit the situation arising out of the shortage of cloth. 'Many friends have told me', Gandhi wrote, 'that the nation is not to expect anything from you [millowners]. They point out the fact that you have not, with one or two honourable exceptions, paid anything to the Tilak Swaraj Fund. . . . The merchants who deal in foreign cloth, and with whom I am pleading [for the boycott of foreign cloth] frightened me by saying that the result of their response will simply mean that you will immediately send up the prices and fling up in the face of the nation the law of supply and demand in support of the inflation of price'.[13]

Gandhi appealed to the industrialists to conduct their business on national rather than purely selfish lines. Their response to his appeal was tepid during the non-cooperation movement. So it was ten years later during the Salt Satyagraha movement. In 1942 during the Quit India movement, they made huge profits from war-contracts while the entire Congress leadership was in prison. Compared with them, the merchants almost throughout India showed a greater spirit of self-sacrifice, by closing their shops and establishments when the Congress called for a hartal, and often (even furtively) contributing to Congress funds. The Indian capitalists were cautious in taking any steps which might bring down on them the wrath of the authorities, and though their association with the nationalist struggle was peripheral, Gandhi did not encourage a 'hate-campaign' against them. With some of them, such as Jamnalal Bajaj, G. D. Birla and Ambalal Sarabhai, he had cordial personal relations. He employed some of them—such as G. D. Birla and Purshotamdas Thakurdas—as counterweights to British capitalist and financial interests in the Round Table Conference in 1931. Jamnalal Bajaj and G. D. Birla generously financed the Mahatma's projects of social and educational reforms, such as the campaigns for eradication of untouchability, promotion of village industries and basic education. Bajaj was basically apolitical in his outlook; but G. D. Birla occasionally appointed himself the Mahatma's spokesman in discussions with the British officials in India and England, who soon discovered that he was not so influential in shaping Congress policies as he posed to be. Birla's published correspondence gives an exaggerated impression of his role in political negotiations. He certainly had access to Gandhi, and his influence was always cast on the side of restraint, on avoiding a confrontation with the Raj, or in favour of seeking a *modus vivendi*, but there were other leaders such as Jawaharlal Nehru and the Congress Socialists who brought a contrary pressure to bear on Gandhi. The fact is that every possible point of view, from the most conservative to the most radical was ventilated in the All-India Congress Committee, and even in the Congress Working Committee. Gandhi listened to everybody, made up his own mind and, on what appeared to him fundamental issues, he did not hesitate to strike out a line even against his closest colleagues. The fact that Birla was Gandhi's host in Delhi or Calcutta does not prove anything. The attitude of the Birla family towards Gandhi was one of deep respect and affection, which was reciprocated. But Gandhi maintained his personal links with individuals irrespective of political or social differences, and there is little evidence to indicate that Birla or his friends were able to get in Gandhi's lifetime any substantial economic gains because of their association with him. Indeed in the framework of the imperialist rule until 1947 Gandhi had no patronage to dispense. The Indian industrialists certainly gained (for example in protective tariffs) from the nationalist pressure against foreign capitalist and financial interests in India; but this was an inevitable by-product of the nationalist movement.

IV

Gunnar Myrdal, who in his *Asian Drama* attempted a painstaking survey of the social and economic scene in India before and after independence, describes Gandhi's message as 'radically egalitarian', and adds that he was 'a true Westernized liberal, indeed a radical and a revolutionary, whose demand for drastic changes in the social and economic order was heard throughout the sub-continent'.[14]

Gandhi's views on the relationship between capital and labour were peculiarly his own, and not quite palatable to Birla and his class. Gandhi called on the capitalists to consider themselves trustees of what they owned, using for themselves and their families only what was essential; they were not to use force against their employees in any circumstances. The workers' unions were also not to use threats of strikes to intimidate the millowners; nor were they to coerce blacklegs. On the distribution of wealth, Gandhi also held radical views. 'The possession of inordinate wealth by individuals', he wrote, 'should be held as a crime against Indian humanity'. He did not see why a millowner, a lawyer, a doctor, a factory worker, or a scavenger should not get the same wages for an honest day's work.[15] The ideal was *equal* distribution, but if this was difficult to achieve, Gandhi called for an *equitable* distribution.[16]

Gandhi's theory of trusteeship was offered as an alternative to both capitalism and communism. It was not a convenient cloak under which the existing system could be justified; on the contrary, it was intended to non-violently redress inequalities and, if necessary, to dispossess recalcitrant owners of wealth.

The trusteeship formula, which Gandhi drafted during his imprisonment in the Aga Khan Palace during the Second World War,[17] did not exclude legislative regulation of the ownership, and the use of wealth for social purposes, and was avowedly a means of transforming the capitalist order into an egalitarian one. If Gandhi did not agree to the forcible expropriation of the rich, it was not because he accepted inequalities as necessary or inevitable, but because he wanted to effect social changes non-violently. Of the apparatus of the modern state he had a deep distrust; 'the really significant choice, as he saw it, lay not between capitalism and socialism, but between centralization and decentralization'.[18] His was essentially the standpoint of the humanist; he hated privilege and monopoly, but he also hated the regimentation and suppression of individual liberty. Through his 'trusteeship' theory, he sought an escape from the dilemma: 'Make men free and they become unequal; make them equal and they cease to be free'.

'I have a vision', Gandhi wrote in 1942, 'that the end of the [Second World] war will also mean the end of capitalism'. 'We may not be deceived', he wrote in 1944, 'by the wealth to be seen in the cities of India . . . . It comes from the blood of the poorest . . . I know village economics . . . I tell you that the pressure from the top crushes those at the bottom. All that is necessary is to get off their backs'.[19] Two years later, he warned that the rich would have to make their choice, 'between a class war and voluntarily converting themselves into trustees of their wealth'.[20] In October 1947, two months after India attained independence, Gandhi declared that the Congress stood for a democratic rule of the peasant, workers and people (*kisan-mazdoor-praja raj*)'.[21] The following month, when J. B. Kripalani resigned from the Congress presidency, Gandhi suggested that the socialist leader, Acharya Narendra Deva should succeed him.

Of one thing, there is no doubt: Gandhi considered political freedom as a prelude to radical social and economic reforms in India, and was furiously thinking of ways to ameliorate the lot of the long-suffering rural masses. During the struggle against the Raj he deliberately soft-pedalled the social issue, but was clear in his mind that the balance had to be redressed in favour of those at the bottom of the social pyramid. 'For years to come', he observed, 'India would be engaged in passing legislation to

raise the down-trodden. If the landlords, the zamindars, moneyed
men, and those who are enjoying privileges—I do not care
whether they are Europeans or Indians—if they find that they
are discriminated against, I shall sympathise with them, but I
will not help them. It will be a battle between the haves and the
have-nots'.[22]

If attitude to property relations is a test of radicalism, Gandhi
would not fail the test. He was, however, a radical in the original
meaning of that much misused word: he went to the root of
every problem. There was hardly any aspect of the human
condition on which he did not think for himself, and come out
with his own, often unconventional, ideas. His approach to his
own profession, that of law, was almost that of a dissident. He
was shocked by the unconscionable delays, the mounting costs
and deep bitterness which litigation generated, and which most
people concerned with the administration of justice, just accepted
as part of the natural scheme of things. While lawyers enriched
themselves, their litigants often faced economic ruin. As a
practising barrister in South Africa, Gandhi encouraged his
clients, wherever possible, to negotiate with their rivals outside
the court. At the same time he did not think it was his duty to
defend a client whether he was right or wrong.

He exhorted the professional classes 'not to make your professions subservient to the interests of your purse . . . . Put your
talents in the service of the country instead of £.s.d. If you are a
medical man, there is disease enough in India to need all your
medical skill. If you are a lawyer, there are differences and
quarrels enough in India. Instead of fomenting more troubles,
patch up those quarrels and stop litigation. If you are an
engineer, build model houses suited to the means and needs of
your people and yet full of health and fresh air'.[23]

Equally unorthodox was the code of conduct which Gandhi
evolved for himself as a political leader in South Africa. Politics
were not for the pursuit of power. He ruled out any personal
gain from public service; he insisted on scrupulous probity in
accounts; he rejected the use of secrecy or questionable means
for even good ends.

Gandhi was a prolific writer and edited journals both in
South Africa and India without commercializing them. He
accepted no advertisements and held that journalism was a
vocation rather than a profession.

Deeply religious as he was, Gandhi rejected the idea of a state religion for India, even though the Hindus formed an overwhelming majority of the population. He was opposed to state aid to religious bodies. 'Religion is a personal matter', he affirmed, 'and if we succeed in confining it to the personal plane, all would be well in our political life'.[24]

Against the abuses of caste and untouchability Gandhi waged an unrelenting war. And on the position of women, Gandhi's views were remarkably similar to those of the leading women reformers. 'Woman is the companion of man', Gandhi wrote as early as 1918, 'with equal mental capacities . . . and she has the same right of freedom and liberty'. His denunciation of such social evils, as child marriage, dowry and purdah, was unequivocal. He advocated equal legal status and the right of vote for women. He would have agreed with the present-day feminists that women must not be treated merely as sexual objects. He believed that women were individuals who should have the freedom to make their own moral choices. It is interesting to recall his comments on the choice of the marriage partner:

> Nor has the society or relatives of parties concerned any right to impose their will upon and forcibly curtail the liberty of action of the young people . . . . Marriage taboos are not universal and are largely based on social usage.[25]

He was prepared to concede the right to divorce to either partner. Only on one point he adopted a position which seemed to his contemporaries, and seems even today impracticable: he opposed the use of contraceptives, and suggested limitation of births through deliberate restraint of married partners.

Gandhi's capacity for creative experiments found expression in the sphere of educational reform. He had always been interested in the teaching of children and had run schools in his ashrams. But in 1937, when he was 67 years old, he was stimulated by Armstrong's book *Education For Life*, and especially its chapter on the 'Education of the Hand', to initiate systematic researches and experiments which culminated in the concept of 'New Education' (*Nai Talim*). One of the important components in this scheme was that of Basic Education, which was designed to impart instruction in schools through useful handicrafts, to harmonize intellectual and manual training and to inculcate dignity of labour and self-reliance.

CHAPTER 16

The Man

Margaret Bourke-White, the correspondent of the *Life* magazine, who was in India during the years 1946–8, and whose last interview with Gandhi took place just a few hours before his assassination, confesses in her book, *Half-way To Freedom* that it took her 'the better part of two years to respond to the undeniable greatness of this man'.[1] To successive Viceroys, Secretaries of State and other British officials, Gandhi remained till the end an enigmatic figure. Part of their difficulty was the 'cultural shock' epitomized in the epithet 'half-naked *faqir*' which Winston Churchill once applied to Gandhi.[2] After all, what were Westerners to make of a political leader, who wore a loin-cloth, drank goat's milk, heard 'inner voices' and announced fasts to solve political problems?

Syed Hossain, an Oxford-trained Indian nationalist, who lived in America in the inter-war years, tells us about a lecture he delivered on Gandhi. After the lecture was over, some one from the audience got up and said: 'Ladies and Gentlemen, we of the Western world cannot follow the leadership of a man who goes about half-naked'. 'The most important thing about Mahatma Gandhi', Syed Hossain replied, 'is not what he wears; the most important thing about Mahatma Gandhi is not even his body; the most important thing about Mahatma Gandhi is his soul. As for the alleged inability of the Western peoples to accept the leadership of someone not conventionally clad, I am reminded that the one whom they call their Master was also clad in nothing more than a loin-cloth at a crucial moment in the history of humanity'.[3]

Curiously enough, some thing of this cultural block, which choked the lines of communication between Gandhi and the people of the West in his lifetime also stood between him and the English-educated classes in India. Lala Lajpat Rai, the fiery nationalist leader from the Punjab, who had joined the non-co-operation movement in 1920, noted that 'such of Gandhi's contemporaries as have drunk deep from the fountains of European history and European politics, and who have developed a deep love for European manners and European culture, neither understand nor like him. In their eyes he is a barbarian, and a visionary and a dreamer. He has probably something of all these qualities because he is nearest to the verities of life and can look at things with plain eyes without the glasses of civilization and sophistry'.[4] Indian radicals, socialists and communists during the nineteen thirties and forties were sharply critical of Gandhi's patient and peaceful methods and visibly chafed under the moral straitjacket that he wrapped upon his followers in the anti-imperialist struggle.

II

Despite his austere life and the saintly halo that he had acquired, Gandhi did not conform to the conventional image of a saint in the Hindu tradition. Raychandbhai, the Jain savant of Bombay and the spiritual mentor of Gandhi during his South African days, had warned him—for the good of his soul—not to involve himself too deeply in the politics of Natal.[5] Many years later, Ramana Maharishi, one of the most venerated Indian saints of this century, remarked that Gandhi was a good man who had sacrificed his spiritual development by taking too great burdens upon himself.[6] Saints are traditionally other-worldly; they help individual 'seekers'; they abhor evil, but leave the problem of coping with it to the ingenuity of the administrators and social reformers. Though Gandhi's deepest strivings were spiritual, he never professed to be a saint. He was not absorbed in philosophical speculation or meditation on the Absolute. Nor did he set much store by cloistered virtue; one had to live and act in the challenging context of social and political life. Horace Alexander, the British Quaker, who saw Gandhi at close quarters, points out that if Gandhi was a mystic, he was 'a very matter-of-fact mystic;[7] no dreamer of heavenly dreams, no visionary, who saw things unutterable when in a state of trance'. When the inner voice spoke to Gandhi, it was only 'to tell him, what to do

tomorrow—how to act more effectively to unite warring communities or how to hasten the end of untouchability'.

Those who accused Gandhi of other-worldliness—and there
were not a few in his own camp, who did so—failed to look
beneath his spiritual idiom. The saintly idiom contained a hard
core of common sense and deep insight into the social realities.
There was much in his cultural heritage, which appealed to
him, but there was also much which repelled him. He had a
strong sceptical streak; even at the age of twenty when, as a
student in England, he was attracted to theosophy, he rejected
its occult lore. As he tells us in his autobiography, he was given
to introspection, and 'at every step carried out the process of
rejection and acceptance'.

Gandhi once described himself as 'an average man with less
than an average ability'. 'I admit', he wrote, 'that I am not
sharp intellectually. But I don't mind. There is a limit to the
development of the intellect, but none to that of the heart'. One
cannot resist the impression that in exalting the goodness of the
heart at the expense of intellectual brilliance, he was fostering
the idea of his own intellectual mediocrity. He was, he said, 'not
built for academic writings. Action is my domain'. He did not
care much for book-learning, but his imprisonments in South
Africa and India enabled him to catch up with his reading, and
what he read, he turned to good account. Even though his
reading was not systematic or regular, it covered a fairly wide
range. Apart from the religious and philosophical works such as
the *Mahabharata*, the *Bhagavad Gita*, the *Upanishads*, the Bible,
the Koran, he studied the writings of Plato, Carlyle, Ruskin,
William James, Gibbon, Adam Smith, Goethe, Buckle, Lecky,
Geddes, Bernard Shaw, Wells, Kipling, Karl Marx and
numerous other writers.

He made it a point to acknowledge his debt to Tolstoy,
Ruskin and Thoreau, but these great Western writers seemed
only to have encouraged him along the path he had already
chosen for himself. And in any case he did not merely borrow
other people's ideas; he transmuted them in a creative fashion.
For example, non-resistance, which to Tolstoy and Thoreau
had been only a means of self-affirmation of the individual,
became in Gandhi's hands an instrument for national self-
affirmation. Ruskin in his *Unto This Last* had expressed inspiring

thoughts which had no relation to the author's life but, which wrought a metamorphosis in Gandhi's life.

It was this capacity for rejection, acceptance, and synthesis which enabled Gandhi to blend the compassionate, intuitive and self-denying elements in his own religious tradition with the constitutional, democratic and secular elements in the Western political tradition. At the same time he discarded the authoritarian and obscurantist elements in his native heritage as firmly as he rejected Western materialism, competitiveness and militarism.

Gandhi did not lay any claim to originality. 'I represent no new truths', he said, 'I do claim to throw a new light on many an old truth'. Nor did he make any pretence to infallibility. Indeed, he described himself simply as one 'who claims to be a humble searcher after Truth, knows his limitations, makes mistakes, never hesitates to admit them'. Though he expounded his ideas on almost every conceivable subject in thousands of articles and letters over a period of more than fifty years, he never tried to build them into a system. What is called Gandhism is, therefore, only a distinctive attitude to society and politics rather than an ideology, 'a particular ethical standpoint rather than fixed formulae or a definitive system'.

During his conversations with Gandhi, Louis Fischer, Gandhi's American biographer, felt that the Mahatma was thinking aloud. 'He did not attempt to express his ideas in a finished form', writes Fischer. 'You heard not only words, but also his thoughts. You could, therefore, follow him as he moved to a conclusion . . . . He was interested in an exchange of views, but much more in the establishment of a personal relationship. Even when evasive Gandhi was frank . . . . His brain had no blue pencil'.[8]

Gandhi was continually developing and outgrowing his own ideas. It was not difficult to confront him with his earlier views on, say, the caste system and the place of machinery in the Indian economy, and point out the discrepancies. When accused of inconsistency, he retorted that he was consistent with truth, not with the past. Scholars and politicians who detect contradictions and paradoxes in Gandhi's views do not make sufficient allowance for the fact that he was engaged in a ceaseless effort to match his deeds with his thoughts and beliefs. Whether or not he succeeded in integrating his insights into his basic beliefs, 'truth to him would have to be revealed in action and in conflict, not in text books'. He had not merely to discover the truth for himself, but to discover the terms—within his ethical framework—on which he could cooperate with others. And since the only authority he could command was moral, and the only means he had was an appeal to the head and the heart, he had to be patient and accept compromises on details in order to achieve his ultimate political and social objectives.

'Life', he said, 'is not one straight road. There are so many complexities in it. It is not like a train which once started, keeps on running'.[9] On another occasion, he said: 'One cannot climb the Himalayas in a straight line'.[10]

Gandhi advised N. K. Bose, the eminent Indian anthropologist, not to depend merely on his writings, but to live with him for sometime, if he wanted to understand him. Bose followed the advice with much profit, and acquired a new insight into Gandhi's humanity and dynamism:

> the secret of Gandhi's greatness lay not in the absence of human failings and foibles, but in his inner restlessness, ceaseless striving and intense involvement in the problems of mankind. He was not a slave to ideas and concepts, [which] were for him aids in grappling with human problems, and were to be reconsidered if they did not work.[11]

III

Gandhi had entered politics in 1894 at the age of twenty-four and for the next fifty-odd years, there was hardly any time in his life, when he was not in the centre of a storm. He seemed, however, to follow Gautam Buddha's dictum that 'by rousing himself, by earnestness the wise man may make for himself an island which no flood can overwhelm'. He acted as his reason and conscience dictated, but was not over-anxious about the results. Even when he was struggling against heavy odds, he would not throw up the sponge. 'Satisfaction lies in the effort', he would say, 'not in the attainment. Full effort is full victory'.

Unlike most politicians, Gandhi did not allow politics to swallow his humanity. Even in the midst of momentous developments, he could find time to wash the sores of a resident leper in his ashram, to dissect the meaning of a verse from the *Gita*, or to answer a letter from an unknown correspondent in a remote corner of India. As a barrister in South Africa he gave not only legal advice to his clients, but instructed them in the best way of weaning a baby or curing chronic asthma. During his first imprisonment in India when a fellow prisoner, an African, was bitten by a scorpian, Gandhi immediately washed his wound, wiped it, sucked off the poison, and treated him until he was cured.

Gandhi's punctuality was proverbial; it was said that he was a slave only to his watch. He rigorously rationed his time, but as Amiya Chakravarty, who was Tagore's secretary for some years, recalls, 'even if Gandhi gave you five minutes, he gave you all of himself: "How is your sister?" He would remember that your sister was ill when you saw him last, perhaps months ago, or "What research studies are you doing now?" He was just as deeply interested in you as your own family'.[12]

In his dealings with his opponents, Gandhi's effort was to break through the 'thought barrier', and to establish a rapport with them. This was not easy; the colonial statesmen in South Africa and the British pro-consuls in India were not free to change the basic policies on racial and imperial issues; it was difficult for them to overcome inherited prejudices, or to act against their own 'constituencies'. Gandhi carried on an eight-year-long ding-dong battle with General Smuts, and when he left South Africa in 1914, Smuts wrote to a friend:[13] 'The saint has left our shores, I sincerely hope for ever'. And yet twenty-five years later, Smuts could write that it had been his 'fate to be the antagonist of a man for whom even then I had the highest respect . . . . Gandhi himself received what no doubt he desired—a short period of rest and quiet in jail. For him everything went according to plan. For me—the defender of law and order—there was the usual trying situation, the odium of carrying out a law which had not strong public support, and finally the discomfiture when the law had to be repealed'.[14] In jail, Gandhi had prepared a pair of sandals for Smuts, who recalled that there was no hatred and personal ill-feeling, and when the fight was over, 'there was the atmosphere in which a decent peace could be concluded'.

Another imperial statesman, Lord Irwin, later Lord Halifax,

who collided head-on with Gandhi during the civil disobedience of 1930, lived long enough to see the leader of the non-violent rebellion against the Raj in a gentler light. In his memoirs, he pays a tribute to Gandhi's courage, humour and sense of fairness: 'He was the natural knight-errant, fighting always the battle of the weak against suffering what he judged injustice. The claims of Indians in South Africa, the treatment of the Indian labourers in the indigo fields in India, the thousands rendered homeless by the floods of Orissa, and above everything the suffering arising from communal hatreds . . . all these were in turn a battlefield in which he fought with all his strength for what was to him the cause of humanity and the right'.[15]

Gandhi's graciousness was not reserved for important people. In December 1931 as his three-month stay in London was drawing to an end, he found time to have tea with the Scotland Yard detective who had been attached to him. Next day, the detective remarked: 'Mr. Gandhi must be the hardest worked man I have ever had to look after, unless perhaps Mr. Lloyd George, when he was Prime Minister during the war; but he is the first one who has ever found time to visit me in my home'.

Despite his asceticism and the aura of saintliness, Gandhi was no killjoy. A globe-trotter and a hard-bitten American journalist, who had rubbed shoulders with political leaders in many countries, found Gandhi a 'very sweet, gentle, informal, relaxed, happy, wise, highly civilized man'.[16] Of his indefinable charm there is a glimpse even in a little book written by Gandhi's first biographer, the Reverend Joseph J. Doke of Johannesburg:

> To my surprise, a small, lithe spare figure stood before me, and a refined earnest face looked into mine. The skin was dark, but the smile which lighted up the face, and that direct fearless glance, simply took one's heart by storm. I judged him to be some thirty-eight years of age, which proved correct . . . . There was a quiet assured strength about him, a greatness of heart, a transparent sincerity, that attracted me at once to the Indian leader. We parted friends . . .[17]

Two years later, in December 1909, Gokhale, Gandhi's friend and political mentor, told the Lahore meeting of one Indian National Congress:

> Gentlemen, it is one of the privileges of my life that I know Mr. Gandhi intimately; and I can tell you that a purer, a nobler, a

braver and a more exalted spirit has never moved on this earth.
Mr. Gandhi is one of those men who touch the eyes of their weaker
brethren as with magic and give them a new vision. He is a man
among men, a hero amongst heroes, a patriot among patriots, and
we may well say that in him Indian humanity at the present time
has really reached its high water-mark.[18]

Gokhale was not given to hyperbole, and was known to
choose his words carefully. Among those who were to immediately
succumb to Gandhi's charm was the young Jawaharlal Nehru,
the only son of an agnostic, affluent and extrovert father, and a
product of Harrow and Cambridge. Nehru's autobiography
makes no secret of the intellectual and temperamental gulf
between him and Gandhi, but he gives some fascinating vignettes
of the Mahatma:

His smile is delightful, his laughter infectious and he radiates
light-heartedness. There is something childlike about him which is
full of charm. When he enters a room he brings a breath of fresh air
with him which lightens the atmosphere.

Gandhi had his foibles and fads, and had developed his own
peculiar ideas on celibacy, diet, health and nature-cure. His
ashram was a human laboratory to which he admitted scholars,
social workers, budding politicians, young radicals and some
cranks. Sometimes he took in even atheists, bigots, former
political terrorists, and men and women who did not seem quite
sane. Questioned why he wasted his time on these people,
Gandhi replied, 'Mine is a mad house, and I am the maddest of
the lot. But those that cannot see the good in these mad people
should have their eyes examined'.

IV

Rabindranath Tagore once described Gandhi as essentially a
lover of men and not of ideas. Gandhi did not ram his ideas
down the throats of other people and made allowances for
human frailties. Richard Gregg, one of his American disciples,
narrates an interesting conversation with him:

We were talking about simple living and I said it was easy for me to
give up most things, but that I had a greedy mind and wanted to
keep my books. He said: 'Then don't give them up. As long as you
desire inner help and comfort from anything, you should keep it. If

you are to give it up in a mood of self-sacrifice, or out of a stern sense of duty, you would continue to want it back, and that unsatisfied want would make trouble for you. Only give up a thing when you want some other condition, so much that the thing no longer has any attraction for you, or when it seems to interfere with that which is more greatly desired'.[19]

Compassionate and compromising as he was, Gandhi's family did not seem to have been the beneficiary of these qualities. In South Africa, as we have seen, his wife found that overnight she had to give up much of the privacy and comfort she had enjoyed as the wife of an affluent barrister, and to assume the role of a farmer's wife and a house-keeper for Gandhi's fellow workers and disciples. She was driven to despair by her husband's refusal to give to their children regular education. He refused to send his sons to missionary schools; he insisted that they learn in their mother-tongue rather than in English even though that would handicap them in their careers; he rated character-building higher than book learning, and had no use for an educational system geared to money-making. His sons had to bear the brunt of his educational ideas; three of them, Ramdas, Manilal and Devdas, survived them, married, and led normal, useful lives, but the eldest, Harilal, rebelled, led an erratic and unhappy existence, bringing much embarrassment and sorrow to his parents.

Gandhi has been called a 'cruel' husband and an exacting father. 'He was', Arthur Koestler wrote, 'as near a saint as anybody can be in the twentieth century; as a father he came as near to the Demon King of the *Bhagavatam* as any western-educated Hindu could be'.[20] There is no doubt that Gandhi's family had to do without much that is taken for granted in upper middle class homes. This was due to the transformation which took place in his life-style in South Africa. He had turned his back on domestic and professional ambitions. His family had also to fit in with the stern code which he had devised for himself as a politician. We have already seen how he had, despite the protests of his wife, declined expensive gifts from his grateful compatriots in Natal. His austerity—like much else what he advocated—began at home, and his family had willy-nilly to submit to it. Indeed, he widened his family circle to include his colleagues and co-workers: he 'belonged to all, and to no one in particular, like a mother in a joint family'.[21]

This explanation of Gandhi's severity towards his family may seem superficial in this post-Freudian age, though it will easily make sense to those acquainted with the cultural milieu in which Gandhi had grown up. Luckily for us, Erikson, the eminent Harvard psycho-analyst, and a pioneer of 'psycho-history' and 'psycho-biography' has probed this theme in some depth. He points to an ambivalence in Gandhi's attitude to sex and family life. 'Clinically, so to speak', Erikson writes, 'there can be little doubt that the idea of basic sin may be much aggravated by personal factors and historical circumstances', and refers to three strands in Gandhi's 'ambivalence'. The first was his early marriage and 'precocious sex life combined with his moral scruplosity, which could not contain and in fact aggravated a sense of sadism in his sexuality'. The second strand was Gandhi's 'aspirations and gifts' which led him into 'a life of service to humanity on a level which called for self-discipline of a high order.' And finally, there was his wife, Kasturba's extraordinary capacity for renunciation which enabled Gandhi to achieve a high degree of self-discipline.

Erikson lays his finger on 'a moral absolutism', which Gandhi used 'as a weapon against his own instinctuality'.[22] He also refers to Gandhi's preoccupation with 'sinfulness', and refusal to recognize the drive behind instinctual satisfaction. Nevertheless, the fact remains—and Erikson underscores it—that Gandhi gained in vigour and agility from these inner struggles and became better equipped for the role he was to play on the political stage. Erikson's clinical analysis of Gandhi's emotional conundrums and crises is merciless, but he cannot withhold his admiration for the end-product of the whole process, and describes Gandhi as 'the wholest of men and one of the most miraculously energetic—most energetic, in fact, when inspired by the very momentum of recovery from temporary self-doubt and inactivation.'[23]

'Gandhi solved for his period in history and for his own people', Erikson says, 'what he could not resolve in his private life'. Gandhi may not have been the most enviable of husbands or fathers, but he 'turned into the father of his nation', and 'extended his paternal feelings to mankind'.[24] To quote an epigram, attributed to Princess George of Greece, an analyst trained by Freud, 'the normal man has yet to be found—*and, when found, cured*'. Gandhi was certainly not 'normal by conventional standards. We can well imagine a 'normal' Gandhi, a prosperous England-returned barrister, living in a bungalow in Santa Cruz in Bombay, educating his children in English schools, dividing his time between the High Court and the Gymkhana Club, playing his rubber of bridge, or his occasional game of golf, writing letters to the Editor of the *Times of India* on vegetarianism, and addressing the Rotary Club on 'nature-cure', and attending—with the Kaiser-Hind medal on his chest—receptions given by His Excellency the Governor of Bombay. Gandhi's wife and children may have had an easier life, but India and the world would certainly have been the poorer for it.

The Message

Gandhi instigated, if he did not initiate, three major revolutions of our time, the revolution against racialism, the revolution against colonialism, and the revolution against violence. He lived long enough to see the success of his efforts in the first two revolutions, but the revolution against violence was hardly under way, when an assassin's bullet removed him from the scene.

Gandhi had worked for the day when violence would be outlawed in inter-state conflicts just as it had been outlawed within the borders of the nation-states. Paradoxically, the stoutest champion of nationalism against imperialism was also an ardent internationalist. As far back as 1924, he had declared that 'the better mind of the world desires today not absolutely independent states, warring against one another, but a federation of friendly, inter-dependent states'.[1]

Gandhi's public life was wholly taken up by the struggles he waged on behalf of his countrymen in South Africa and India. He had turned down proposals to visit other countries; he felt he could not really recommend his method to the world, until he had shown its efficacy in his own country. In 1934, when his name was suggested for the Nobel Peace Prize by the *Christian Century*, his comment was characteristic: 'Do you know of a dreamer who won attention by adventitious aids?'[2]

Gandhi had no illusions about the ready acceptance of his method by nation-states, armed to the teeth. Even in his own country, and in his party there were sceptics, who insisted that force would only yield to force. He was asked again and again whether there was any precedent in history of love conquering hatred, and of non-violence triumphing over violence. His answer was that 'History was only a record of every interruption of the even working of the force of love':

> Two brothers quarrel; one of them repents and re-awakens the love
> that was lying dormant in him; the two again begin to live in peace;
> no body takes note of this. But if the two brothers, through the
> intervention of solicitors or some other reasons, take up arms or go
> to law . . . their doings would be immediately noticed in the press,
> they would be the talk of their neighbours and would probably go
> down to history. And what is true of families and communities is
> true of nations. There is no reason to believe that there is one law
> for families and another for nations.[3]

There were periods, when Gandhi was unable to sustain his
campaign against the Raj at a high pitch because of the massive
repression launched by the British authorities. But he neither
abandoned his goal, nor his method. He remarked once that his
satyagraha campaigns usually passed through five stages:
indifference, ridicule, abuse, repression and respect. And when
a campaign survived repression, it 'invariably commanded
respect, which is another name for success'.[4]

The initial acceptance of Gandhi's method in India had been
due to the fact that he offered an alternative to constitutional
agitation and terrorism, both of which had failed to make a real
dent on the imperialist structure in India. Though Gandhi
believed his method was capable of universal application, he
used it sparingly. He did not dispense satyagraha as a panacea
for quick relief; it was a drastic remedy for the resolution of
social and political conflicts; it took into account human greed,
passion and irrationality; it did not eliminate possibilities of
injury or death; it did not guarantee a successful conclusion.
There could be loss of life among those who dared to plunge into
the non-violent battle; in that case it did not follow that non-
violence did not work. Millions of lives had been lost in world
wars, and yet the rulers of nations had not come to the conclusion
that violence had failed to work.

It is easy to forget that war has been the lot of mankind
throughout recorded history; even the last century was no
exception. Between 1861 and 1965, it has been estimated, there
were no less than 50 wars between nation-states, and 43 imperial
and colonial wars, and 27 million combatants were killed. And
throughout this period (except for some 25 years) some sort of
inter-state war was in progress. In most of these wars, the
aggressor tended to have an edge over his opponents because he

could choose when and where to strike; he could also get away with fewer casualties and some territorial gains. The development of nuclear weapons has, however, altered the conditions of war. It has made nonsense of Clausewitz's dictum that war is a continuation of diplomacy by other means. Wars in the past may have helped in the aggrandisement of the victors, but as things are today, there are going to be no victors. For the Americans or for the Russians, to dream of a world empire through conquest is absurd. To attack another nation would amount to attacking oneself, and the right of retaliation would mean no more than the right to compound the catastrophe. There will not be much of a world for the winner—if there is any—to enjoy; the price of victory would be intolerably high.

II

The Super Powers are not unaware of the risks of an all-out confrontation; as J. K. Galbraith puts it, the word 'detente' has simply come to mean a 'no suicide pact'. Nevertheless, nuclear disarmament is nowhere in sight, and the huge arsenals of conventional and nuclear weapons have failed to give a sense of security to the main antagonists. Disarmament conferences have been part of the international scene since 1932—having been interrupted only during the Second World War. The negotiations, which have alternately raised and belied hopes, have been concerned with temporary reduction of a particular armament, such as bombers, naval ships or nuclear missiles. Agreement has been difficult to attain because of mutual suspicion and distrust. Each country has its own perception of its vulnerability; it is not easy to balance a particular weapon against another. How many tanks are to be set off against bombers, or what conventional forces would be considered a quid pro quo for nuclear war-heads? Then there is always the fear, that the 'enemy' may succeed in evading the curbs embodied in the agreement. A biological convention, which permits research, or a nuclear-test-ban treaty, which permits underground tests, are poor safeguards against disaster. The fact is that there are no technical solutions for psychological problems.

In a climate of suspicion and fear, nations seem to be inexorably swept along a tide which their rulers are unable to control. Einstein, who as a physicist, and as a correspondent of President Roosevelt, had been indirectly associated with the making of the nuclear bomb, recalled later 'the ghost-like character of this development, in its apparently compulsory trend. Every step appears as the unavoidable consequence of the preceding one'. J. Robert Oppenheimer, the distinguished American physicist, said in 1956: 'We did the devil's work'. When he was asked as to why he had first opposed and then agreed to the production of the hydrogen bomb, Oppenheimer's answer was characteristic: 'When you see something that is technically sweet, you go ahead, and you argue about it only when you have had your technical success'.

In his *Civilization and Its Discontents*, Freud had argued that civilization was a socially necessary framework for repressing the instinctual life of man; out of this repression flowed discontents which gave scope to man's aggressive, destructive 'death instinct' to erupt into the barbarism of war. Freud was not very optimistic about the possibilities of controlling this self-destructive instinct. 'There is no likelihood of our being able to suppress humanity's aggressive tendencies', he wrote in an open letter to Einstein who had asked him publicly whether there was 'any way of delivering mankind from the menace of war.' In an earlier book, *Beyond The Pleasure Principle*, Freud had written that the deepest instinctual drive in every form of life was the drive to revert to the original state of inorganic matter—of nothingness. He went so far as to suggest that the purpose of all life was death.

Gandhi would not have accepted this dismal view of human destiny. He conceded that 'in our present state we are partly men and partly beasts', but he affirmed that man's nature was not essentially evil, that 'brute nature has been known to yield to the influence of love'. His was a doctrine of original goodness. He did not divide mankind into good and bad; there were only evil acts, no wholly evil men. For him the 'moral solidarity of mankind' was an ever-present fact: 'We are all tarred with the same brush, and the children of one and the same Creator, and as such the divine powers within us are infinite'.[5]

It was on these premises that Gandhi evolved his method of satyagraha. In his hands it was a sophisticated weapon, rich in moral overtones. He paved the way for his non-violent campaigns carefully, improvised his tactics to suit the changing situation, and kept the door open for conciliation and settlement with the adversary. He chose men of high intellect and moral calibre as his lieutenants, and enforced a stern discipline on his followers. These elements have been missing in many of the campaigns launched since his death. Strident propaganda, massive strikes and demonstrations by themselves do not add up to satyagraha; to obstruct or thwart the opponent without the complex and compassionate approaches of Gandhi is to miss the spirit of his method.

The critical issue today is whether Gandhi's method can be adopted for resisting external aggression. Gandhi affirmed that it could be. During the Second World War, he wrote articles recommending it to the Abyssinians, the Czechs and the Poles. After the war he lived for less than three years, and these were exceptionally turbulent years in India, whch taxed his energies to the utmost. He had thus no opportunity of experimenting with his method in international conflicts. However, the record of his struggles on the national stage contains useful insights for those who would like to pull mankind back from the edge of disaster. In 1957 Sir Stephen King-Hall, a noted military strategist, took a leaf out of Gandhi's book, when he suggested in a lecture to the Royal United Service Institute of England, that the possibilities of non-violent resistance should be officially investigated as part of a viable defence of Great Britain. Sir Stephen's book *Defence in the Nuclear Age* sold well, and was translated into several languages. He recognized that Gandhi had left no readymade strategies for defence against external aggression, and the theoretical bases for non-violent resistance would have to be sought in his experience in India and South Africa: 'There were broad ideas and principles which could help in developing defence methods and techniques'. The object was not to defend particular buildings or borders, but the whole society with its own way of life. This might need total non-co-operation with the aggressors by the civil service, industry, trade unions, schools, universities, the press, radio and television, and the church of the nation which was attacked.

'Civil Defence' has come to be recognized in recent years as a serious, if unorthodox, proposal in the field of national defence alternatives. Interest by individual military strategists has grown, and the defence departments of some of the smaller countries, especially in Scandinavia, have begun to consider possibilities of non-violent resistance, but these ideas are still in the stage of exploration, and have not yet become the strategies of nations and their rulers.

III

A serious complication in the struggle for world peace is (in the words of Hannah Arendt) that 'the problems of modern war and of modern tyranny must, if either is to be solved, be faced simultaneously'. But this aspect of the fight for peace further strengthens the case for the non-violent method, as it can be invoked equally against tyranny at home and aggression abroad. The solutions for these problems in terms of non-violent techniques would have to be found by each country according to its cultural and political conditions. Gandhi never claimed finality for his ideas; he did not have all the answers. In his struggle for human rights and the political liberation of his country, he was ceaselessly experimenting. He once described satyagraha as 'a science in the making'. It is possible that the theory and practice of non-violence are today at the same stage of development as electricity was in the days of Marconi and Edison.

When Gandhi denounced industrialism and militarism before the First World War few people took him seriously. Indeed, right through the Second World War, his pleas for renunciation of violence were dismissed as the outpourings of a visionary. It was only when the atom bomb revealed the Frankenstein that the very perfection of industrialism and militarism had created, that Gandhi's message acquired a new relevance and urgency.

Soon after the bombing of Hiroshima and Nagasaki in 1945, when Jawaharlal Nehru went to see him, Gandhi closely questioned him about the atom bomb; its manufacture, its capacity to kill and poison, its toll of Japanese cities. Gandhi listened to Nehru silently, and then (in Nehru's words) 'with deep human compassion loading his gentle eyes', remarked that this wanton destruction had confirmed his faith in God and non-violence, and that 'now he [Gandhi] realised the full significance of the holy mission for which God had created him and armed him with the *mantra* of non-violence'. Nehru recalled later[6] that, as Gandhi uttered these words, he had a 'look of revelation about his eyes', and that he resolved then and there to make it his mission to fight and outlaw the bomb.

Gandhi was not destined to launch a crusade against nuclear warfare. He was assassinated in January 1948. In the following year, when Nehru visited the United States he related his conversation with Gandhi to Einstein. With a twinkle in his eyes, Einstein took a pad and pencil, and wrote down a number of dates on one side, and events on the other, to show the parallel evolution of the nuclear bomb and Gandhi's satyagraha respectively—almost from decade to decade—since the beginning of the twentieth century. It turned out that by a strange coincidence while Einstein and his fellow scientists were engaged in researches which made the fission of the atom possible, Gandhi was embarking on his experiments in peaceful, non-violent satyagraha in South Africa; indeed, the Quit India Struggle almost coincided with the American project for the manufacture of the atom bomb.

The choice between these two opposite and parallel strategies, epitomized by the atom bomb and Gandhian non-violence, which Einstein noted in 1949, has become even more critical today. One wonders whether the instinctive death-wish of our species (which Freud perceived) would triumph over the 'soul-force' which Gandhi sought to evoke in the human breast. Gandhi himself had no doubt that peace 'will not come out of a clash of arms, but out of justice lived and done by unarmed nations in the face of odds'.[7]

Notes

CHAPTER 1

THE GANDHI FILM

1   Richard Grenier, 'The Gandhi Nobody Knows', *Commentary*, March 1983, p. 71.

CHAPTER 2

'A HINDU OF HINDUS'

1   Richard Grenier, op. cit., pp. 12–13.
2   *Harijan*, 28 September 1935.
3   'What Gandhi's religious thought offers is by no means an eclectic package, but a challenge to think through and live through the breadth and depth of opportunities for sharing whatever worldly goods or those deepest intimations which are the warp and woof of life. So understood religion can once more become a binding force which goes beyond national frontiers and which sees no barrier between one community and another.' Margaret Chatterjee, *Gandhi's Religious Thoughts* (London, 1983), p. 181.

CHAPTER 3

THE MAKING OF THE MAHATMA

1   George Orwell, *Collected Essays: Journalism and Letters of George Orwell* (London, 1978 edn), p. 523.
2   *Harijan*, 7 July 1946.
3   Ibid., 15 June 1947.
4   Quoted in *India Today*, 31 May 1983.
5   'In *Mundaka Upanishad* it is said that we can attain the self by truth, control, spiritual fervour and absolute extinction of all sex desires. Only the sages who have purged themselves of all moral defects and faults are capable of perceiving this holy spiritual light within themselves.' S. N. Das Gupta, *Hindu Mysticism* (Delhi, 1976 edn), p. 56.

'How infinitely superior is the joy of God to the pleasures of "woman" and "gold"! To one who thinks of the beauty of God, the beauty of even Rambha and Tilottama (two celestial dancing girls of exquisite beauty) appears as but the ashes of a funeral pyre. No spiritual progress is possible without the renunciation of "woman" and gold.' Ramakrishna, quoted in *The Gospel of Ramakrishna* (Madras, 1957), pp. 334–5.

'Without having Sannayasa none can really be the knower of Brahman—this is what the Vedas and Vedanta proclaim. Don't listen to the words of those who say, "We shall both live the worldly life and be knowers of Brahman." That is the flattering self-consolation of crypto pleasure-seekers . . . . Highest love for God can never be achieved without renunciation . . .' Vivekananda, *The Complete Works* (Mayavati Memorial edn, Calcutta, 1956), Vol. 6, pp. 504–5.

6 Erik H. Erikson, *Gandhi's Truth* (New York, 1969), p. 237.

7 Gilbert Murray, 'The Soul as it is, and How to deal with it', *The Hibbert Journal*, January 1918, pp. 191–205.

8 Lloyd and Susanne Rudolph, *The Modernity of Tradition* (London, 1967), p. 249.

9 Erikson, op. cit., p. 403.

10 Ibid., pp. 404–5.

11 N. K. Bose to H. D. Sharma, unpublished letter, 26 June 1956.

12 *Harijan*, 24 February 1940.

13 'The ideal towards which I believe we should move is best described by the term "androgyny". The ancient Greek word *andro* (male) and *gyn* (female) defines a condition under which the characteristics of sexes and the human impulses expressed by men and women are not rigidly assigned. Androgyny seeks to liberate the individual from the confines of the appropriate.' Carolyn G. Heilburn, *Toward a Recognition of Androgyny* (New York, 1974), p. x.

14 N. K. Bose, *My Days with Gandhi* (Calcutta, 1974), p. 175.

CHAPTER 4

GANDHI AND THE CASTE SYSTEM

1 E. Stanley Jones, *Mahatma Gandhi* (London, 1948), p. 143.

2 N. Mansergh and P. Moon (eds), *Transfer of Power* (London, 1977), Vol. VII, pp. 144–7.

3 Ibid., Vol. VIII, p. 170.

4 Ibid., pp. 466–8.

5 *Young India*, 8 December 1920.

6 *Harijan*, 16 November 1935.

7 Ibid., 25 March 1933.

8 *Yervada Mandir* (Ahmedabad, 1945), p. 32.

9 *Harijan*, 16 November 1935.

10   Ibid., 25 July 1936.

11   Tibor Mende, *Conversations with Nehru* (Bombay, 1958), p. 25.

CHAPTER 5

THE FIGHT AGAINST RACIALISM

1   *Washington Post*, 18 April 1983.

2   Quoted in Gandhi's Open Letter of December 1894 to members of the Natal legislature, *Collected Works of Mahatma Gandhi* (Ahmedabad, 1969), Vol. I, p. 185.

3   Extract from despatch of 6 November 1913 to Colonial Office by Governor-General of South Africa, *Collected Works of Mahatma Gandhi*, Vol. XII, p. 593.

4   *Young India*, 12 January 1928.

5   Thomas Karis and Gwendolen M. Carter (eds), *From Protest to Challenge: A Documentary History of African Politics in South Africa 1882–1964* (Stanford, 1972), Vol. II, p. 62.

6   Ibid., Vol. I, p. 268.

7   Ibid., Vol. II, p. 69.

8   Ali A. Mazrui, 'Gandhi, Marx and the Warrior Tradition', *Journal of Asian and African Studies*, Vol. XII, 1977, pp. 193–4.

9   Fergus Macpherson, *Kenneth Kaunda of Zambia: The Times and the Man* (Lusaka and London, 1974), p. 105.

10   Interview with the author on 26 January 1975, Oral History Transcript, Nehru Memorial Museum and Library.

11   Martin Luther King, *Stride Toward Freedom* (London, 1959), p. 91.

CHAPTER 6

AMRITSAR, 1919

1   Paul Johnson, 'Gandhi Isn't Good For You', *Daily Telegraph*, 16 April 1983; Algernon Rumbold, 'Film, Facts & History', *Encounter*, March 1983.

2   O'Dwyer to Chelmsford, 23 April 1919, Chelmsford Papers.

3   Home Political A, August 1919, No. 261–72, National Archives of India.

4   C. H. Setalvad, *Recollections and Reflections* (Bombay, 1946), p. 311.

5   Algernon Rumbold, *Watershed in India 1914–1922* (London, 1979), p. 203.

6   Rupert Furneaux, *Massacre at Amritsar* (London, 1963), p. 179.

7   Valentine Chirol to Chelmsford, 5 January 1921, Chelmsford Papers.

CHAPTER 7

THE TWO FACES OF IMPERIALISM

1   John Vincent, 'We Must Not Feel Guilty Over Gandhi', *Sun*, 21 April 1983.
2   Percival Spear, *Twilight of the Mughals* (Cambridge, 1951), p. 218.
3   Ibid., p. 219.
4   Edward Thompson and G. T. Garratt, *Rise and Fulfilment of British Rule in India* (London, 1934), p. 462.
5   Ibid., pp. 454–5.
6   Ibid.
7   Henry Cotton, *Indian and Home Memories* (London, 1911), p. 65.
8   M. Darling, *Apprentice To Power* (London, 1966), p. 116.
9   Jawaharlal Nehru, *An Autobiography* (London, 1958 edn), p. 71.
10 B. R. Nanda, *Gokhale, Indian Moderates and the British Raj* (Delhi, 1977), p. 178.
11 Judith Brown, 'War and Colonial Relationship' in D. W. C. Ellinwood and S. D. Pradhan (eds), *India and World War I* (Delhi, 1978), p. 25.
12 *Foreign Quarterly Review*, April 1844, p. 217.
13 Sir Richard Temple, *Cosmopolitan Essays* (London, 1886), p. 187.
14 *Edinburgh Review*, January 1858, quoted in George D. Bearce, *British Attitude Towards India* (London, 1961), pp. 242–3.
15 *The Mahratta*, 4 July 1897.
16 D. G. Karve and D. V. Ambekar (eds), *Speeches and Writings of Gopal Krishna Gokhale* (Bombay, 1967), Vol. III, pp. 295–6.
17 Home Department, Judicial, August 1880, 203–5, National Archives of India.
18 Hardinge to Carmichael, 2 August 1912, Hardinge Papers.
19 Amiya Kumar Bagchi, *Private Investment in India 1900–1939* (New Delhi, 1980), p. 420.
20 For Gokhale's evidence, see *Indian Expenditure Commission*, Vol. 3; *Minutes of Evidence taken before the Commission on the Administration of India* (London, 1900).
21 Fleetwood Wilson to C. Dilke, 9 November 1909. Fleetwood Wilson Papers.
        In a letter to the Bishop of Calcutta, dated 22 June 1913, Wilson wrote: 'Surely, God never turned India into a grazing ground for the overflow of the middle class of England with no thought of lifting up of those committed to our charge'.
22 Philip Woodruff, *The Men Who Ruled India, The Guardians* (London, 1955), p. 20.
23 Ibid., p. 17.

CHAPTER 8

THE 1917 DECLARATION

1   *Daily Telegraph*, 6 April 1983.

2 Algernon Rumbold, *Watershed in India 1914–1922* (London, 1979), p. 100.

3 Letter of 17 May 1888 to the editor of *Morning Post*, Allahabad, quoted in S. R. Mehrotra, *India and the Commonwealth* (London, 1965), p. 33.

4 Lord Curzon, *The Place of India in the Empire: Being an Address presented before the Philosophical Institute of Edinburgh on 19 October 1909* (London, 1909).

5 Edward Thompson and G. T. Garratt, *Rise and Fulfilment of British Rule in India* (London, 1934), p. 536.

6 G. T. Searle, *The Quest for National Efficiency* (Oxford, 1971), pp. 30–1.

7 Lamington to Morley, 6 April 1906, Lamington Papers.

8 B. Fuller, *Studies of Indian Life and Sentiment* (London, 1910), p. 339.

9 Home Political, Deposit, June 1909, No. 3, National Archives of India.

10 Minto to Morley, 27 February 1907, Morley Papers.

11 Quoted in *India*, 29 December 1906.

12 12 H.L. Deb. 5s., Coll. 155–6.

13 Hardinge's minute, 1 July 1912, commenting on the secret memorandum of R. Craddock, Hardinge Papers.

14 Hardinge to Clarke, 27 March 1913, Hardinge Papers.

15 S. Lee, *King Edward VII: A Biography* (London, 1927), Vol. II, p. 385.

16 Quoted in *New India*, 14 July 1916.

17 Algernon Rumbold, op. cit., pp. 96–7.

18 Earl of Ronaldshay, *The Life of Lord Curzon* (London, 1928), Vol. III, p. 166.

19 P. Robb, 'The British Cabinet and Indian Reform 1917–19', *Journal of Imperial and Commonwealth History*, 4, 3 (1976), p. 331.

20 Edwin S. Montagu, *An Indian Diary* (London, 1930), p. 10.

CHAPTER 9

GANDHI AND THE RAJ

1 Home Political, B, 141–147, May 1919.

2 As implied in D. A. Low, 'The Government of India and the First Non-Cooperation Movement 1920–1922' in R. Kumar (ed.), *Essays on Gandhian Politics* (New Delhi, 1971), p. 298.

3 Gandhi to H. S. L. Polak, 30 May 1919, Gandhi Papers.

4 Algernon Rumbold, *Watershed in India, 1914–1922* (London, 1979), p. 294.

5 Ibid.

6 R. J. Moore, *The Crisis of Indian Unity* (Delhi, 1974), p. 315.

7 Ibid., 154.

8 R. J. Moore, *Churchill, Cripps and India, 1939–45* (Oxford, 1979), p. 26.

9 Penderal Moon (ed.) *Wavell, The Viceroy's Journal* (Delhi, 1977), p. 33.

10 R. J. Moore, op. cit., p. 138.

11   Sir William Vincent, the Home Member, on 20 June 1919 wrote: 'I have discussed this matter with Sir William Marris [Home Secretary] and the Director of Central Intelligence. My own feeling is that Gandhi is losing influence, and he knows it, and that may make him in a moment of despair to secure martyrdom and public sympathy. We should as far as possible give him no opportunity of attaining his object.' Home Political A 261–272, August 1919.

12   Quoted in Stanley Jones, *Mahatma Gandhi* (London, 1948), pp. 127–8.

13   William L. Shirer, *Gandhi: A Memoir* (London, 1981), p. 16.

14   B. R. Nanda, *Mahatma Gandhi: A Biography* (London, 1958), p. 335.

15   Ibid., p. 336.

16   Gandhi to C. R. Das, telegram, 8 April 1919, Gandhi Papers.

17   Rafi Ahmed Kidwai to Jawaharlal (undated), Nehru Papers.

18   William L. Shirer, op. cit., p. 62.

19   'It is its [the British Government's] great secret and character that when it does wrong, it seems to justify itself before the world on moral grounds.' Gandhi to Private Secretary to the Viceroy, 7 July 1917, Gandhi Papers.

20   'It was during these years that the issue was settled, whether India's independence was to be trodden in argument or in blood.' Algernon Rumbold, op. cit., p. 317.

21   R. J. Moore, op. cit., p. 4.

22   Malcolm Muggeridge, *Chronicles of Wasted Time*, Vol. II: *The Infernal Grove* (London, 1973), p. 25.

23   On 8 October 1943, Wavell, who was coming out to India as Viceroy to succeed Linlithgow, called upon Prime Minister Churchill and recorded in his diary, 'P.M. was menacing and unpleasant when I saw him at 3 p.m. . . . and indicated that only over his dead body would any approach to Gandhi take place. I think . . . he is determined to block it [any political advance] so long as he is in power.' Penderal Moon, op. cit., p. 23.

24   *Encounter*, March 1983, p. 63.

25   A. J. Toynbee, 'A Tribute' in *Mahatma Gandhi: 100 Years* (New Delhi, 1968), pp. 375–6.

26   Quoted in William L. Shirer, op. cit., p. 71.

CHAPTER 10

RELIGION AND POLITICS

1   H. Montgomery Hyde, *Lord Reading* (London, 1967), p. 352.

2   B. R. Nanda, *Mahatma Gandhi: A Biography* (London, 1958), p. 211. Tilak's letter reproduced in *Young India*, 28 January 1920.

3   B. R. Nanda, *Gokhale, Indian Moderates and the British Raj* (Delhi, 1977), p. 170.

4   Dennis Dalton, 'Gandhi and Roy: The Interaction of Ideologies in India' in Sibnarayan Ray (ed.), *Gandhi, India and the World* (Melbourne, 1970), p. 166.

5   *Harijan*, 22 September 1946.

6   Louis Fischer, *Life of Mahatma Gandhi* (London, 1951), p. 430.

7   C. F. Andrews to Gandhi, 12 March 1933, Gandhi Papers.

8   Jawaharlal Nehru, *An Autobiography* (London, 1958 edn), pp. 370–1.

CHAPTER 11

GANDHI AND THE PARTITION OF INDIA

1   *Sun*, 21 April 1983.

2   Quoted in A. H. Albiruni, *Makers of Pakistan*, p. 109.

3   Earl of Minto, *Speeches* (Calcutta, 1910), pp. 65–70.

4   Harcourt Butler to Erle Richards, 16 September 1906, Butler Papers.

5   There is plenty of evidence of this in the Fazl-i-Husain Papers in India Office Library. Also see R. J. Moore, *The Crisis of Indian Unity* (Delhi, 1974), pp. 192–3.

6   S. R. Mehrotra, *Towards India's Freedom and Partition* (New Delhi, 1979), p. 226. Also see B. R. Nanda, *Gokhale, Gandhi and the Nehrus, Studies in Indian Nationalism* (London, 1974), pp. 136–41, P. Hardy, *The Muslims of British India* (Cambridge, 1972), pp. 224–5.

7   Khalid B. Sayeed, 'The Personality of Jinnah and the Political Strategy' in C. H. Philips and M. D. Wainwright (eds), *The Partition of India* (London, 1970), p. 276.

8   *Tribune*, 2 July 1937.

9   'The idea of Pakistan has set the Muslim imagination afire. They see strange, undreamed of, limitless possibilities in it. They imagine Pakistan to be a state in which men shall be free from oppression, injustice and exploitation, and free from selfish greeds, covetness and fear of poverty.' F. K. Khan Durrani, *The Meaning of Pakistan* (Lahore, 1946), p. 117.

10 In the annual session of the Muslim League in 1938, there was a reference to the promotion of Muslim interests through an alliance with the British. Jinnah's comment was characteristic: 'I say the Muslim League is not going to be an ally of anyone, but would be the ally of even the devil, if need be in the interests of Muslims'. A pin-drop silence suddenly appeared to seize the House at this stage. Mr. Jinnah paused for a moment, and then continued: 'It is not because we are in love with imperialism; but in politics one has to play one's game as on the chess-board.' Jamil-ud-din Ahmad, *Speeches and Writings of Mr. Jinnah* (Lahore, 1946), Vol. I, p. 78.

11 Khalid B. Sayeed, op. cit., p. 283.

12 Khaliquzzaman, *Pathway to Pakistan* (Lahore, 1961), p. 397.

13 P. Hardy, *The Muslims of British India* (Cambridge, 1972), p. 164.

14 R. J. Moore, *Escape from Empire* (London, 1983), p. 284.

15 *Harijan*, 6 April 1940.

16 Ian Stephen, *Pakistan* (London, 1964), p. 101.

17 R. J. Moore, op. cit., p. 159.

18 Sudhir Ghosh, *Gandhi's Emissary* (London, 1967), p. 180.

19 S. R. Mehrotra, op. cit., p. 232

20 R. J. Moore, 'Jinnah and the Pakistan Demand', *Modern Asian Studies*, 1983, pp. 560–1.

CHAPTER 12

THE PARTITION MASSACRES

1 *Indian Annual Register*, July–December 1946, p. 226.

2 Ibid., p. 178.

3 N. K. Bose and P. H. Patwardhan, *Gandhi in Indian Politics* (Bombay, 1967), p. 7.

4 Pyarelal, *Mahatma Gandhi: The Last Phase* (Ahmedabad, 1956), Vol. I, p. 470.

5 W. H. Morris-Jones, 'The Transfer of Power, 1947—A View from the Sidelines', *Modern Asian Studies*, 16, 1 (1982), pp. 1–32.

6 N. Mansergh and P. Moon (eds), *India, The Transfer of Power, 1942–47* (London, 1980), Vol. IX, Document No. 138.

7 *Partition Proceedings* (Expert Committee No. 1), Government of India, Vol. I, p. 81.

8 Y. Krishan, 'Mountbatten and the Partition of India', *Journal of Historical Association*, University of Glasgow, February 1983, p. 35.

9 *Collected Works of Mahatma Gandhi*, Vol. LXXVIII (Ahmedabad, 1979), p. 414.

10 Pyarelal, op. cit., Vol. II, p. 382.

11 Tariq Ali, *Can Pakistan Survive?* (London, 1983), p. 96.

12 Khalid B. Sayeed, 'The Personality of Jinnah and the Political Strategy' in C. H. Philips and M. D. Wainwright (eds), *The Partition of India* (London, 1970), p. 293.

13 Ibid.

14 Y. Krishan, op. cit., p. 36.

15 'As in Mediaeval Europe, the feelings of the masses were fed almost exclusively by religious food; that is why to provoke a strong movement it was necessary to present to the masses their own interests in religious clothes.' Marietta Stepaniants, 'Development of the Concept of Nationalism—The Case of the Muslims in the Indian Sub-Continent', *The Muslim World*, Vol. LXIX, January 1979, p. 36.

16 Sir Francis Wylie, the Governor of U.P., wrote to the Viceroy on 29 August 1946 that 'the most ominous feature of the [Muslim League] demonstrations was the notable tendency to give the whole movement a religious flavour. Many of the meetings took place in and around mosques just after the usual Friday prayers. I am told too that members of the Muslim League party are making vigorous efforts to obtain support of Maulvis and Imams everywhere in the province. You might have noticed that *Dawn* recently started quoting extracts from the Quran every day on its leader page . . . . There has been some shouting of slogans about "Jehad" in various towns here . . .' N. Mansergh and P. Moon, op. cit., Vol. VIII, pp. 342–3.

Sir Khizr Hyat Khan, Prime Minister of the Punjab, told the Viceroy in April 1946: 'The Muslim League had liked to keep the idea [of Pakistan] vague, so that every Muslim might interpret it as a sort of utopia where his own ambitions would be satisfied. At the elections [in February 1946], they had identified it [Pakistan] with Islam, the Koran and the Holy Prophet.' N. Mansergh and P. Moon, op. cit., Vol. VII, p. 148.

17 Francis G. Hutchins, *Spontaneous Revolution: The Quit India Movement* (New Delhi, 1971).

CHAPTER 13

GANDHI AND NON-VIOLENCE

1 *Washington Post*, 18 April 1983.

2 M. K. Gandhi to P. Desai, 15 November 1914, Gandhi Papers.

3 N. Mansergh and E. W. R. Lumby (eds), *Transfer of Power* (London, 1971), Vol. II, p. 346.

4 B. Shiva Rao, 'India 1925–47' in C. H. Philips and Mary Doreen Wainwright (eds), *The Partition of India* (London, 1970), p. 429.

5 M. K. Gandhi to Miraben, 31 May 1942, in *Bapu's Letters to Mira* (Ahmedabad, 1949), pp. 360–1.

6 N. Mansergh and P. Moon (eds), *Transfer of Power*, Vol. V, p. 64.

CHAPTER 14

MAN versus MACHINE

1 R. Palme Dutt, *India Today* (Bombay, 1947), pp. 506–7.

2 B. N. Ganguli, *Gandhi's Social Philosophy* (Delhi, 1973), p. 312.

3 *Harijan*, 16 November 1934.

4 R. K. Karanjia, *The Mind of Mr. Nehru* (London, 1960), p. 52.

5 P. C. Joshi, 'Gandhi and Nehru' in B. R. Nanda and V. C. Joshi (eds), *Studies in Modern Indian History* (New Delhi, 1972), p. 123.

6 See Gunnar Myrdal, *Asian Drama* (London, 1968), Vol. II; B. N. Ganguli, op. cit.; P. C. Joshi, op. cit.; Amritananda Das, *Foundations of Gandhian Economics* (New Delhi, 1979); Raj Krishna, 'The Nehru-Gandhi Polarity and Economic Policy' in B. R. Nanda et al., *Gandhi and Nehru* (New Delhi, 1979).

7 P. C. Joshi, op. cit., p. 132.

8 A. H. Huq, 'Economics of Growth and Employment: The Gandhian Approach', *Gandhi Marg*, January 1981, p. 576.

CHAPTER 15

A REACTIONARY

1   Roy blamed the failure of the non-co-operation movement on the 'class character of Gandhi's leadership . . . as he sacrificed the movement to the two forces of landlordism and industrialism'.

In July 1924, Roy wrote that 'the defeat of orthodox Gandhism is complete and final . . . and Mr. Gandhi as leader of Indian national struggle has sung his swansong . . .' *Documents of the History of the Communist Party of India*, Vol. 2: *1923–5*, p. 411.

2   In his *Social Background of Indian Nationalism* (first published in 1943), A. R. Desai wrote that 'Gandhism had met both the needs of the national bourgeoisie viz., that of exerting pressure on imperialism through mass struggle, and second, that of limiting that struggle, diverting it in those channels which also would [*sic*] make it harmful for Indian propertied classes.'

3   Richard Grenier, 'The Gandhi Nobody Knows', *Commentary*, March 1983, p. 62.

4   *Harijan*, 27 May 1939.

5   William L. Shirer, *Gandhi: A Memoir* (London, 1981), p. 60.

6   *Harijan*, 5 December 1936.

7   Ibid.

8   *Harijan*, 2 January 1937.

9   Louis Fischer, *A Week With Gandhi* (Bombay, 1944), pp. 72–3. Jawaharlal Nehru was present during this conversation between Gandhi and Fischer.

10 B. N. Ganguli, *Gandhi's Social Philosophy* (New Delhi, 1973), p. 245.

11 N. K. Bose, *Studies in Gandhism* (Calcutta, 1962 edn), p. 36.

12 P. C. Joshi, 'Gandhi and Nehru' in B. R. Nanda and V. C. Joshi (eds), *Studies in Modern Indian History* (Delhi, 1972), p. 131.

13 *Bombay Chronicle*, 6 July 1921.

14 Gunnar Myrdal, *Asian Drama* (London, 1968), Vol. 2, p. 754.

15 N. K. Bose, op. cit., p. 88.

16 Ibid., p. 86.

17 Shriman Narayan, *India Needs Gandhi* (New Delhi, 1976), pp. 12–3.

18 Amlan Datta, 'Aspects of Gandhian Economic Thought' in Sibnarayan Ray (ed.), *Gandhi, India and the World* (Melbourne, 1970), p. 257.

19 *Amrita Bazar Patrika*, 30 June 1944.

20 D. G. Tendulkar, *Mahatma* (Delhi, n.d.), Vol. 7, p. 47.

21 M. K. Gandhi, *Delhi Diary* (Ahmedabad, 1948), p. 69.

22 B. N. Ganguli, op. cit., pp. 261–2.

23 *Young India*, 15 November 1931.

24 *Harijan*, 31 August 1947.

25 Ibid., 29 May 1937.

CHAPTER 16

THE MAN

1 Margaret Bourke-White, *Halfway to Freedom* (Bombay, 1950), p. 184.

2 'It is alarming and also nauseating to see Mr. Gandhi, a seditious Middle Temple lawyer, now posing as a faqir of a type well-known in the East, striding half-naked up the steps of the Viceroy's palace while he is still organizing and conducting a defiant campaign of civil disobedience to parley with the representative of the King-Emperor . . .' R. R. James (ed.), *Winston Churchill: His Complete Speeches* (London, 1974), Vol. V, p. 4985.

3 Syed Hossain, *Gandhi, The Saint as Statesman* (Los Angeles, 1937), p. 44.

4 Raghavan Iyer, *The Moral and Political Thought of Mahatma Gandhi* (New York, 1978), pp. 6–7.

5 D. K. Bedekar, *Towards Understanding Gandhi* (Bombay, 1975), p. 86.

6 Raghavan Iyer, op. cit., p. 380.

7 Horace Alexander, *Consider India* (London, 1961), p. 75.

8 Louis Fischer, *The Life of Mahatma Gandhi* (London, 1951), p. 406.

9 C. Shukla, *Conversations of Gandhi* (Bombay, 1949), p. 10.

10 *Collected Works of Mahatma Gandhi*, Vol. XIV, pp. 515–16.

11 P. C. Joshi, 'Gandhi and Nehru: The Challenge of a New Society' in B. R. Nanda et al., *Gandhi and Nehru* (Delhi, 1979), p. 41.

12 Interview with Amiya Chakravarty, Oral History Transcript, Nehru Memorial Museum and Library, New Delhi, p. 15.

13 W. K. Hancock, *Smuts: The Sanguine Years 1870–1919* (Cambridge, 1982), p. 345.

14 S. Radhakrishnan (ed.), *Mahatma Gandhi: Essays and Reflections* (London, 1939), p. 278.

15 Lord Halifax, *Fulness of Days* (London, 1959), pp. 148–9.

16 Louis Fischer, op. cit., p. 397.

17 Joseph J. Doke, *M. K. Gandhi: An Indian Patriot in South Africa* (Madras, 1959), p. 9.

18 *Report of the Twenty-Fourth Indian National Congress*, 1909, pp. 88–9.

19 Richard Gregg, quoted in *Manas*, September 1981, p. 7.

20 Arthur Koestler, *The Lotus and the Robot* (London, 1960), p. 145.

21 Erikson, 'In Search of Gandhi' in *Philosophers and Kings: Studies in Leadership* (Bombay, 1968), p. 35.

22 Erikson, *Gandhi's Truth* (New York, 1969), p. 250.

23 Ibid., p. 378.

24 Interview with Erikson, *Span Magazine*, New Delhi, November 1983, p. 13.

EPILOGUE

THE MESSAGE

1   Gandhi's presidential address at the Belgaum Congress in *Congress Presidential Addresses, From the Silver to the Golden Jubilee*, Second Series (Madras, 1934), p. 745.

2   Paul F. Power, *Gandhi on World Affairs* (London, 1961), p. 132.

3   M. K. Gandhi, *Indian Home Rule* (Ahmedabad, 1938), p. 79.

4   Raghavan Iyer, *The Moral and Political Thought of Mahatma Gandhi* (New York, 1978), p. 308.

5   M. K. Gandhi, *An Autobiography* (Ahmedabad, 1945 edn), p. 337.

6   R. K. Karanjia, *The Philosophy of Mr. Nehru* (London, 1966), pp. 60–1.

7   Roy Walker, *The Wisdom of Gandhi* (London, 1943), p. 57.

Index